How NOT to Be a Miserable Cow

Alison Capra

ALISON CAPRA

How NOT to be a Miserable Cow

"Neicy" 1986 #enjoythejourney

DEDICATION

This book is dedicated to my mother. The most selfless, free-spirited women I've ever known. She taught me what it means to work hard, love people, and truly enjoy the journey. Your smile is infectious your laugh is contagious, and you light up every room you walk into. Every word that I wrote was inspired by your voice in my head, teaching me How NOT to be a Miserable Cow. It is my aspiration in life to be more like you every single day. I love you, mom.

CONTENTS

PROLOGUE

Wild Thing 2002 #hotmess

I am a pastor's daughter so as you can imagine I had some wild oats to sow before I figured my life out. I spent half of my teenage years dancing on tables, acting out, and the other half doing missions trips all over the world – it was a gypsy's life in terms of freedom and experience. I slept in the jungles of Brazil, rode safari in Africa, and built daycares for children in Belize. I don't even know if I understood what type of person I was, or that I was truly enjoying my youth. I just think as a young person I didn't have a care in the world and I was determined to live my life to the fullest, EXPRESS myself, and have a GOOD TIME!

By the time I graduated college I was engaged to my first husband-to-be. You see, I wanted to have everything figured out way too fast. I had known my fiancé since junior high and although he wasn't my "first love", he liked me and I liked him, so despite everyone's disapproval we got hitched at 19. Too young to comprehend what I was choosing, completely oblivious to red flags and well, reason; I wanted to "sort things out" so I could "start living" the life I was positioning for myself.

11.14.04 Wedding #1

What you need to understand is that my first husband was not just handsome. In fact, beautiful is probably the only word that could properly describe his outward appearance. Like a young Leonardo

DiCaprio, he had a sexy smile and my grandma used to say he was too handsome for his own good. Looking back, she was absolutely correct. However, I wasn't able to see clearly and I completely overlooked his gnarly and broken past. It feels like I walked directly into a MAC truck when we got married.

My first husband was controlling, demeaning and abusive to say the least. Two years in and I was looking for a way to find an out. I used to lie in bed and wish he would cheat on me so that I could leave him and save face. But he didn't and I had to buckle up and make some big girl decisions. Our fights had escalated past breaking things and punching holes in walls. When things got physical between us I tried to be gone as much as possible: out with friends, extra work, even church. My inner gypsy was pulling me away from the relationship. I used to imagine myself moving to Brazil and living in the jungle in a big treehouse. All day long I would fantasize about becoming a war reporter in the Middle East and just living in some hostel with a camera and rolls of film to develop (haha developing film, that's cute). I would hide my wedding ring or take it off so I didn't have to answer questions about my poisonous relationship. I would leave the country on mission trips with my family as often as I could. Nothing was enough because as soon as we were home alone together again, it always turned nasty. To this day, I have haunting, tormenting dreams that I never left and I am back, trapped with him, running from room to room trying to get out the door just so I can run to safety. He used to take all the car keys and torment me in the house for hours. It was this kind of disturbing behavior that people never saw.

My mom used to try to counsel us. She would say, "If you two don't take care of each other, someone else will." and she was right. I was looking for an escape and I eventually found one. My life didn't improve much and about 47 terrible decisions later, there I was, up shit creek without a paddle, broke, depressed and alone with a disgusting pack-a-day habit, working 70 hours a week at a bar to pay two mortgages and an apartment. This was so far from that carefree gypsy life I was longing for. At one point, my hundreds of dollars in electric bills caught up with me in the dead of winter and they cut my power off. Just like that. I didn't even think they could do that. As I was lying there in my pitch black apartment, wearing everything I could find to keep myself warm, wrapped in covers, taking shots of cinnamon whiskey, watching my own breath, all I could think about was how bad HE had fucked me. It wasn't fair. A stream of questions ran through my mind:

Why did this happen to me?

How did this loser come into my life?

Why did I marry him?

Bottom line: it was all his fault. This hauntingly beautiful man that everyone told me was prince charming... why had I believed them? I spent the next few years of my twenties loathing him and feeling sorry for myself. I was wishing the worst on him every day, telling everyone what a disgusting human being he was. I was the biggest victim of them all. I deserved better. I deserved happiness.

Meanwhile, I was looking around at all these women with families and careers and awesome lives. I literally remember saying: "How do these girls do it? How do these girls marry so well that they don't have to do anything but sit on their ass and watch their dreams come true?" I was so naïve in SO many ways. It is only now in my thirties that I am able to recognize my own blatant stupidity. I married a teenager from a broken home. His mother and grandmother committed suicide while he was in their care. His father was a drug addict and abandoned him. He was passed around from family member to family member. He had a record, and oh yes, a drug problem. I knew ALL of these things when I married him and in that sense, I was not really a victim. In some ways, I had become a miserable cow. I have a picture of myself on my 25th birthday. In the picture, I'm trying to cover up my pain with a "sexy smile", but it's so obvious that behind the mask, I was lost, struggling with depression and anxiety. The dark circles under my glossy eyes were a visceral indicator I was using drugs and alcohol to deal with abuse and the pain from my divorce. I was feeling so broken.

Even though, I was in a terrible, abusive relationship with a person who had the emotional intelligence of a snail, I realized that it had been my own choice to marry him and stay in the relationship. When I married him, nobody had forced me and I stayed with him 4 years too long. Period. Every choice I made before, during and after my first marriage had been my own and sadly, these decisions had led to my own demise. I had chosen to stay miserable and I literally let my husband beat me down for way too long.

What I have later realized is that I am not a victim. And neither are you. We are not entitled to success or even love from others. We are not entitled to an easy life. And we are not even entitled to happiness. Bad things happen every day to good people. Choices and mistakes are made that affect everyone around us. In the meantime, we are responsible for our emotional well-being. We are all responsible for cultivating happy and love-filled lives. I strongly believe that happiness isn't something you pursue and find by chance, but something you cultivate every single day with every single decision you make.

This book is a very personal guide to love and happiness. It tells you what I've learned about How NOT to be a Miserable Cow as well as the story of how I've found my way through two marriages and a ton of bad decisions. My road from being a miserable cow to creating a and fulfilling life for myself.

CHAPTER 1
ANATOMY OF THE MISERABLE COW

Let me start by painting you an all too familiar picture. We've ALL been there. Sitting across the table from our favorite friends. Everybody is swapping stories, sharing wine and great food next to our significant others. We are reveling in the fact we are having adult conversations and not bound to a desk or a pile of shitty diapers; enjoying a night out and savoring the moments in front of a fire pit with our feet up with fewer worries than we had the very same morning. We even start to ask ourselves, "Why do I get so stressed out? My life is pretty damn good." The liquid lubricant has relaxed our mind, bodies, emotions and even our speech.

And then, almost like clockwork, it happens. The female counterpart in this sketch, after approximately 2.5 glasses of wine, with a look of disgust, begins to sour faster then that protein shake you left in your car on a hot day. As her facial expressions begin to turn, you can hear the tone of her voice change. Like a loose cannon, it's almost as if the alcohol has lit a fuse and she is going to implode from the inside out. She begins to dissect her husband's every word and thought, every detail of every story, down to the sentence and suddenly even the breathing pattern of her husband makes her sick. We've all been around these couples that were seemingly in love and now barely stand the sight of one another. We might even be one of those couples. However, the sour comments are only the beginning. Soon, the nagging kicks in: **"Well SOMEBODY doesn't like to help taking the kids to school".** Now your own skin is beginning to crawl from sheer embarrassment for your friends. The night has changed for everybody, but this woman is on a roll and she is going in for the kill. Velvet daggers begin to cut through the atmosphere like butter. There is no possible way she could emasculate her counterpart any further unless she pulled down his pants and publicly flogged him at the dinner table. What has happened to your friend? Can she hear herself? An overwhelming sense of disgust drives you away from their company. No one is able to get away fast enough. What did you just witness? It's what I call a "miserable cow".

It's easy to identify a miserable cow when you see one. The miserable cow has this heifer mentality of nagging, bitching and complaining about everything surrounding her everyday life so much so that even the people around her become miserable. The misery is contagious and infectious. The miserable cow is usually an angry, bitter individual, who is resentfully blaming everyone around her for her empty and lonely life. I know, this sounds harsh, but stay with me. The classic example is the self-destructing old lady alone in an apartment full of cats. But lots of people die angry and alone every day without having cultivated a life of creativity and happiness.

I don't think there is an exact formula that transforms a free-spirited young woman to an unhappy and bitter individual. People make mistakes. We all have baggage. And I can assure you I will never insist that I have all of the answers.

But on my personal quest for growth, I have identified within our culture one major flaw... the miserable cow. In this chapter, I'm going to go over the anatomy of the miserable cow. Then I will follow up on these traits in the next few chapters. I am going to address how you have become a miserable cow in the first place. Overall, I truly believe that the number one way that this transformation happens is that people - especially women, become creatively insecure. Instead of doing things that they love, like developing themselves and developing a skillset and well, growing. They start to become insecure and then start projecting their insecurities on others. The insecurity is often sparked by a bad relationship or some other draining element in their life. They might start playing the victim role and think that everything bad happens to them all the time. It's a mental perspective issue. The next few chapters are going to be giving you some tough love. You might even want to put the book down because it's hard to admit that you have some of this miserable bovine mentality. I know it was hard for me! But rest assured, because there is one thing I'm certain of: Not ALL men are assholes and not ALL women are crazy. Somewhere in the middle, we have the ability to create healthy, meaningful relationships if we are willing to collect less and work through more. It is my hope that this book can help each of us to identify the habits, thoughts and behaviors that are making us miserable; work through them, and start cultivating a happy life. I hope that every reader will challenge him- or herself to release pain from the past and find new ways to create a life of purpose, love and happiness. I truly hope you can create a meaningful legacy and a healthier perspective for yourself and the people you love.

So let's get down to business on the anatomy of a miserable cow so that you can identify if you are in fact a miserable cow. Perhaps you just want to identify "a friend" as a miserable cow. Others might argue differently when it comes to the specific characteristics of the miserable cow because there are so many varieties, but these are the traits I personally have come across the most:

COW TRAIT #1: Resting Bitch Face

The first trait is physical and it's not hard to spot: pursed lips, furrowed brows and sunken cheeks. It's the resting bitch face and it's an all too familiar condition among miserable cows. According to the Urban Dictionary, Resting Bitch Face occurs "when a person, usually a girl, naturally looks mean when her face is expressionless." The face comes with an ever-present gnarly attitude. If your friends are constantly asking you what's wrong, you might have resting bitch face. I would suggest you go get that checked out. Or, you know, if you're not interested and like your face that way then you might as well stop reading and I'll send you some wrinkle cream samples because you'll need them.

Resting Bitch Face #RBF

The resting bitch face has made the beauty industry money for decades in the form of Botox treatments and anti-wrinkle creams. This also means that the resting bitch face often becomes the most expensive of the miserable cow traits. Trust me, I know, I have had a lot of Botox.

What's truly amazing about resting bitch face is that it comes so naturally when you are unhappy. Most of the time, you won't even realize that you've developed it until you catch a glimpse of yourself in the mirror. There you are thinking you look all beachy and cute with no make-up on, but in reality you look like you're dying of influenza. The real problem is when you start feeling entitled to this sour expression. If I had a nickel for every girl that told me: "that's just my face", I would be able to pay for a lot more of that damn Botox.

Don't get me wrong; we can all muster up a look of disgust when some twat-waffle cuts us off in afternoon traffic. But that's not what I'm talking about. What I'm referring to is the permanent facial expression that exudes how repulsed she is by her life. In some ways, resting bitch face requires no extra energy for the miserable cow. It might just be that the look portrays no emotion except contempt. This absence of expression itself portrays a lack of interest in everyone and everything around ONESELF. Almost as if you couldn't care less how you make others around you feel. A real miserable cow can wear a resting bitch face at all times without any effort. Let me tell you, Mona Lisa has nothing on a miserable cow. The rest of us usually only get that unpleasant appearance occasionally and we will notice how it always puts us in a bad mood. I still catch myself with a resting bitch face from time to time, but it's not like it used to be. I recently have noticed that when someone takes my picture, I don't have to look fake anymore. It's not a mask. For the first time in my life, I'm right where I belong. I'm enjoying life, working out and utilizing my body to live life to the fullest every day. I have to be honest and say that I'm still struggling with the pain from my past. It's so important to recognize that photos can be fake and they are just a reflection of what we want others to see. Behind the picture is a real life where you have to take care of yourself and choose to be happy.

TRAIT #2: Velvet Daggers –

The Conversational Soft Kill

It's an art really. To insert an insult so clean, so smooth, that the untrained eye might not be able to identify the wound. What is a velvet dagger? I am so glad you asked. Velvet dagger is a military term for "soft kill". We are talking about a quick, smooth, penetrating insult that one might not have even recognized had the victim not been bleeding out dead on the floor. The skillful miserable cow waits for just the right moment, when the target is most vulnerable with ribs exposed for a sharp, quick attack. It takes a long time to develop such skillfulness. The dagger is often pulled out for the first time during a fight with her significant other. Because she knows this other person so well, it's not difficult to find something to say that will hurt deeply. Women are usually physically weaker (than the strongest man) and that has taught us to use words to defend ourselves. As time goes by and the woman develops into a miserable cow, she is so caught in her miserable life that she feels the need to make everybody else miserable. The daggers become sharper for every successful attack. Her husband is constantly walking around wounded which just makes her want to attack him even more. What started as a defense mechanism in nasty fights has now become a personality trait. And the target is no longer just her partner, but everybody around her that makes her feel bad about her life. The victims in these equations are most often just people enjoying their lives because... "How dare they?" In her darkest moments, the miserable cow might even utilize velvet daggers on herself in her destructive and insecure self-talk. Words that were meant to be used to communicate her feelings and dreams are now deadly weapons in her hands. In other words, if words are your weapon and you are always waiting for the perfect time to shatter someone's soul… You MIGHT be a miserable cow.

This definitely does not mean that you need to avoid fights. As a hot-blooded Italian gypsy who is married to a Greek alpha male, we have our fair share of fights. Recently, Nick (my husband) and I have had some big fights over a big business purchase that was going to double our workload. To him, the purchase seemed like a great opportunity that came just at the right time, but to me it seemed like a potentially exhausting endeavor that we didn't have time for at all. I was not pleased because I felt like we were already doing too much and this would just put us over the edge. However, what was going on through these fights was communication. Nick was trying to get me to see his vision and I wasn't letting him. I usually do not say no to Nick. For two reasons really, because #1. I know he is a dreamer and a visionary. #2. I'm not big on the CONTROL-OTHERS sort of vibe. If someone wants to do something bad enough, and you try to stop them, you're only adding fuel to their fire, and my Nicholas… is a man on fire! But my gypsy mindset was worried that this business purchase would tie us down and prevent us from traveling. In fact, a few years ago, when we first started our relationship all he ever talked was selling everything and moving us into a van just to drive down all of the coasts and surf. Nothing aroused my free-spirit more! We haven't gone on our big surfing adventure yet, but we DO travel a lot. I was worried this dream was going to turn into a distant memory. So no matter what he said or did, I just DIDN'T want to get "talked-in" to this purchase. I put up walls, I battened down the hatches. And I geared up for war. I was completely closed off to good, healthy communication. I would say anything to make sure I had my way. But all these random little signs kept appearing along the way. Signs that made it almost frightening for us NOT to move ahead with the purchase. I realized I needed to stop. I needed to stop fighting for my own way; I needed to stop living in fear. We ended up going through with the purchase because we made them an offer and they DIDN'T refuse. The week before I finally caved I made a comment in "jest" over a glass of wine... If you offer them $$ (insert ridiculously low amount) and they take it... then, I guess, it was meant to be. Nick was extremely confident that this was an amazing opportunity, and they came back with a "yes" to our very low offer. An offer that was about

$40,000 less than what they had asked for. And let's just say, I shut my big fat mouth and started working on websites. I'm by no means saying that this went perfectly smooth, or that I ever really "gave in", but let's just say I learned that I needed to resist the urge to get nasty in these fights and from now on, I know to wait and listen before I react. I'm always watching myself to make sure I'm not going in for the soft kill when communicating with my man or anybody else.

Kansas City 2017 #WTF

COW TRAIT #3: Constant Nagging

The squeaky wheel gets the grease. We've all seen it, polite requests are ignored and that is negatively reinforcing that nagging and bitching gets the job done. We've all done it: nagging our partner relentlessly to take out the garbage.

Here's a thought. Do it your fucking self. You expend 3 times the amount of energy nagging someone to put trash outside as you would if you just handled it. And you'd be far less miserable without the knock down drag you're about to have over garbage. It's really not worth it. I understand; it would be great if your partner were also your fulltime housekeeper. But he is not. And at the end of the day, you will probably get sick of some spineless shadow of a man who is begrudgingly handling household chores because you threw a temper tantrum. You both have a life beyond the chores of the house so just take responsibility for something as simple as the trash so that you will be able to look yourself in the mirror and know that you aren't a nagging bitch. Choose your battles wisely.

Nagging is sort of like a pest bite or a rash. It's constantly there and driving you crazy. Do you really want to be a rash-like presence in your partner's life? Constant nagging will literally make your partner feel disdain for your presence. No one wants to be around a nag. Just handle things that need to be handled and move on about your business. You're not entitled to anything so stop acting like you are. If you are feeling taken for granted, communicate those feelings in a healthy respectful way.

I once had a roommate that would only sweep half of the fucking floor in the living room, and then come report to me what she had accomplished and request that I fulfill my half of the obligations. Not only that, but when I had spent hours preparing a meal for both of us she would unload half of the dishwasher afterwards and she would announce: "Since you made dinner I went ahead and did half of the dishes." She did this constantly. Anyone with children knows that that isn't the way it works in a household. If you're going to clean… You're fucking cleaning until the job is done. When I sweep, I sweep the whole floor. Her attitude bothered me because it was a sign of some general feelings of entitlement. It was a way for her to make sure that she never gave too much of herself. I don't know what made her that way. Maybe her parents had acted that way around her, or maybe she had been taken advantage of at some point in her life. Whatever had happened to make her such a nagging person was also making her feel like a miserable cow to be around. Her nagging was affecting me and everybody around her in a negative way. I also believe that it was making her more miserable. I believe that there are two main ways to be happy: either you change your situation or you change your attitude to the situation. When it comes to simple things like unloading a full dishwasher, taking the trash out or sweeping, it's so easy to just take matters into your own hands and change the situation. If the trash smells horrible, then take it out! So few things in life are easy to change so enjoy the fact that you have control over the situation. And if you truly need help battling the chores at home, don't be that miserable cow that nags – just ask politely for help like you would ask your best friend. You can delegate chores and responsibilities as much as you want, but life happens, so roll with it. If you are willing to let the fucking garbage turn you into a nagging sourpuss, then you are literally choosing to be unhappy out of entitlement or laziness. You might want to consider living alone because you are a miserable cow.

COW TRAIT #4: A Steady Stream of Complaints

Complaining is essentially like nagging, but worse because it's not directed at anyone. It's just spewed out and keeps around long enough to pollute the air with negativity. If you find people are pulling away from conversations with you, it's probably not because your breath stinks… it's because your attitude stinks. If you can't contain the way you feel on a regular basis and if you feel the need to draw attention to yourself by complaining... you might be a miserable cow. That fun and light atmosphere when you're hanging out with a good friend immediately disappears when the complaining starts. It drains both of you. It's not just because it's negative, it's also because it doesn't lead anywhere. If you don't like something, then keep it to yourself. If you are ready to face that dislike and move forward, then by all means, share it and we can move forward for you to become a happier and better person.

There are of course many levels of complaining: from complaining about little things that don't matter to complaining about your entire life. Common to all of this is that nobody really wants to hear you repeat how terrible something is. We've all been sitting next to a miserable cow on a beautiful day at the beach and all she can talk about is that "it's so hot!" We get it! It's hot! It's the same temperature for everybody actually. But the rest of us are choosing to focus on the fact that it's Saturday, we are relaxing on the beach with friends, and a dip in the water will cool us down easily. We are living life to the fullest, but she is too busy complaining to see how good her life is. She might even keep the constant stream of complaints going throughout the day. And she probably does have some very annoying things going on in her life. We absolutely understand how much it sucks that you have a headache, you wish your stomach was flatter and you don't like your mother-in-law. We all have problems like that, but we try to keep moving forward.

Am I saying that you should never express your feelings about difficult situations? Absolutely not! It's important to have people to share with. But complaining without any solution is just whining. You are only adding misery to an already negative situation. It becomes a downward spiral of misery where you talk about it so much that it starts to consume your entire life and you forget about all the good stuff. You also get so addicted to the attention you get from complaining that at some point, you don't even look for a solution anymore. You just sit there with your terrible attitude and wallow in your own misery. In the meantime, you make the rest of us either feel bad for you or you suck us into this unpleasant habit of complaining. Trust me, it's infectious. And it's hard to cut out of your life once you've started.

COW TRAIT #5: Jealousy – *the Green-Eyed Monster*

I have a rule when it comes to my friends. No one really knows about it except my life partner, and well now, YOU! The rule is that if a friend or acquaintance EVER starts a sentence with "Oh my gosh, I'm so jealous" of anything they hear or see me do in life... we are no longer **close** friends. This might seem harsh, but it has kept me far away from miserable cows for the past many years. This is because most miserable cows spend a lot of time being jealous of everybody else's life. The jealousy comes from a deep, dark place inside them. It's where they keep their creativity and their dreams. They tell themselves that they are stuck, but then when someone else succeeds or gets lucky, it reminds them of all the goals they aren't pursuing. It hurts and this comes out as jealousy. That ugly, green-eyed monster that makes everybody uncomfortable.

I don't know what kind of person raised you if you haven't learned to be happy for your friends. You might not be unhappy. You might just have a chip on your shoulder. But it comes down to this: if you are incapable of rejoicing with your happy friends when something wonderful happens to them, then you are definitely a miserable cow at some level or another. When they get a promotion, take an expensive trip, win $100, hell, even get laid then be happy for your friends. Use that positive energy to fuel your own life. If you feel a tinge of jealousy creeping in, just remember, you're human, so it's completely natural to feel that way. Instead, just practice saying this when you hear good news: "OMG I am so happy for you." It's the only way to pierce the green-eyed monster right dead in the eye. Force yourself to be happy for your friends. And then when you get home, think about why this specific news made you jealous. Do you need to work harder at your job so that you can earn a promotion? Do you need to work more on your relationship so that you can start getting laid again? Whatever it is, let your friend's good fortune be an inspiration. Stop trying to dissect their life and focus on your own shit.

How to recognize jealousy in a miserable cow? If you can't be happy for your friend and it leaves you with a bitter taste when you get good news about your friends then you are probably experiencing the curse of the green-eyed monster. Think about this quote: *"A creative man is motivated by the ability to achieve, not by the desire to be others."* Stop comparing your life to other people's lives.

Get out of the rat race and give up on trying to keep up with the Joneses. Focus on your own goals and stop being a miserable, jealous cow.

COW TRAIT #6: Entitlement – the Belly of the Cow

I've mentioned entitlement a few times already because it just seems to the core of what's wrong with the miserable cow. It's the belly of the cow and everything is connected to it. The definition of entitlement is a feeling or belief that you deserve to be given something. The sense of entitlement ranges from upset little kid to psychological complexes. It has even been linked with narcissism and borderline personality disorder. Yikes! That's some serious stuff.

I'm going to venture a guess that everyone born in the U.S.A. is guilty of feeling entitled from time to time. In fact, thinking that ANYONE owes you ANYTHING, for ANY reason is a good indication that you are feeling entitled. This is a very, lush, nasty and moist breeding ground for the transition into a miserable cow. Comparing yourself and what you have to what others have is a surefire way to discontentment. Feeling entitled to what others have is even more dangerous.

Dissatisfaction is a nasty little word. While we all want to work hard, strive to do our best in life and achieve wonderful things; that isn't the way that it always works out. Life isn't fair. The truth is, YOUR feelings are NOT the most important thing on earth. Only those with emotional intelligence and a sense of gratitude can properly identify the harsh reality that the feelings and emotions they are having are a chemical reaction to a conditioned perspective brought on by a consistent negative thought pattern. GET YOUR HEAD OUT OF YOUR ASS. Do mothers get rewarded for ruining their bodies, sleepless nights, countless meals, clean-ups, and endless work? No, each special moment that they share with their children is a gift. And such is life. NO ONE owes you anything. Look at EVERY good thing that happens to you as a gift, and not a reward. Do you feel it is for certain that you deserve better? Do you feel like you owed respect and preferential treatment? If you do, you're in the belly of the cow.

The anatomy of a miserable cow would not be complete without the sense of entitlement. Cows believe they are entitled to whatever they want. They believe that for some reason they DESERVE to have what others have; that because there are nicer options available for cars, dresses, husbands, you name it, they are entitled to them. When they don't have the best looking life in the cul-de-sac they become discontent in many, if not all, areas of their lives. When this happens, they will easily take their dissatisfaction out on those closest to them. For decades we have watched commercials and seen ads portraying females as nagging, griping and dissatisfied creatures. We all laugh and think it's funny. But is it actually? Do we want our children to see us as ungrateful and disrespectful? I know I don't. In a culture with a thriving democracy (well, sort of) it seems that we have accepted and unleashed the miserable cow. These cows all want a judge to tell them what's fair. They will hire an expensive lawyer to build a case to bring to the jury in order to incriminate and vilify anybody who has wronged them. They want to justify their actions because they feel and act like victims, and they are obsessed with being right. If that's you; if you feel entitled to a happy life, then you are probably a miserable cow and you need to keep reading. In the next few chapters, I'm going to walk you through how this has happened to you and to many other women in our generation. I will talk about the two biggest factors: discontent and possessiveness. I promise you it will get a little ugly.

However, don't despair. We are going to turn this around. Turn your weakness into your strength and focus on cultivating a happy life.

Kenya #meaningoflife

CHAPTER 2

The Culture of Discontent

Ali 2008 #SinCity

"There is no currency for contentment, but just imagine the wealth we could attain if we simply chose it for ourselves." — unknown

According to the Mayo Clinic, 70% of Americans are taking prescription drugs. Anti-depressants and opioids are among the top prescribed drugs in the U.S. Behind the counter of every small-town pharmacy you'll find walls lined with orange, red and green bottles filled with the perfect elixir for what ails you. Take a pill when you're down, a Xanax when you're up. It can be something to take the edge off or something so you can simply check out. What does this say about our country? It shows that there are a lot of miserable cows walking around out there. And common to all of them is that they want to FEEL better, but they don't know how. So in a culture where it is so easy to just pop a pill, that becomes their coping mechanism. We are even encouraged to deal with our problems that way when the authorities in society, such as doctors, consider it the best treatment to prescribe drugs when people complain about life.

This is absolutely not a book that wants to condemn people for taking and abusing prescription medication. I have fallen into this trap more than once in my life. I felt like the only escape from my personal pain was to numb it. I remember feeling so displaced in my second marriage. I had become what felt like a live-in nanny to 3 little boys (whom I adored) and a full time support staff to a husband with severe depression. His sadness was a dark cloud over our entire home. He isolated himself and he wanted to isolate me from the outside world as well. He hated other people and never wanted to leave the house. I spent my days trying to work and contribute to household expenses and my nights trying to keep a family from drowning in sadness. When I went to get my wisdom teeth out, they gave me a bottle of pills and it seemingly took away all of my pain and left me comfortably numb. I spent the next few months doing everything I could to get more pills since they helped me escape my own emptiness for the first time in months.

I'm not one to judge anybody; not the people taking drugs and not the people behind them. This is not an outcry to bash pharmaceutical companies for making drugs, or even the doctors who overprescribe these drugs, or the hospital and company executives who line their pockets with the dividends. Instead, I am hoping that I can help each of us identify one of the most silent, but deadly physiological killers of them all: discontent.

Miserable cows have a lot of problems. What makes discontent one of the biggest issues? Mainly, it's because it's such a big problem that people don't even know where to start. They know that something is off because they wake up unhappy every morning. But it's hard to figure out exactly what. They might think it's because their husband isn't giving them enough attention, their kids are struggling in school, their friends are leaving them out of girl's nights, they don't have a good workout routine, their boobs aren't big enough, or because their house doesn't look like a Southern Living magazine ad. Maybe they are too close to the problem to realize that they are discontent with their life overall. And this affects every little part of their day, from the way they approach work to the way they greet their family at the end of the day. I am sure there are a million different contributing factors to the emotional dissatisfaction in our culture and in the lives of all these miserable cows. But here are my top 5 reasons why you are discontent:

REASON FOR DISCONTENT #1:
You are comparing.

If you are struggling with feelings of discontentment or dissatisfaction in your own life, I have one recommendation: get off social media for as long as it takes for you to feel happy again. While we all enjoy surfing and sharing on social media, and some of us need it for work and business, Facebook is the number one place for people to compare their life to the lives of those they follow. Comparing is, by definition, to estimate, measure, or note the similarity or dissimilarity between one thing and another. When it comes to your life, comparisons aren't as easy as they seem. I'm a photographer and for the past 14 years I have taken wedding and family photos for hundreds of people. Trust me, no one is as happy or as beautiful as they portray themselves to be on social media. In reality, people show up with their messy hair, their damaged marriage and their tantrum-throwing kids, I take the pictures and then I edit them. A lot, sometimes. When it comes down to it, I can give you a smaller waist, bigger bust and perfect skin. I can even make sure everybody is smiling at the same time. And that's what people are looking for when they hire a professional photographer. They want someone to remove their flaws and show them the way they wish they looked. Then they post these pictures on social media along with some sweet caption that is supposed to portray how great their life is. However, for each great picture I capture, I have ten times as many of screaming children, angry wives, bitter mother-in-laws, and shitty dogs, but those pictures aren't lucrative for my photography business so I keep them to myself. People share what they want you to see. We all do it. Myself included. They post that split-second of being a perfect couple or family that I managed to capture. In the meantime, you have first row seats to the chaos that is your own life. That's just not a fair comparison. So if you are unable to look at photos without comparing your life to the fake lives on social media, JUST GET OFF! It will do you good.

I am not saying that social media is the root of all evil. I use it a lot to promote business and to communicate with people. In some ways, something like Instagram has given a lot of creative people an outlet for their artistic dreams. And I fully support that. But contributing and posting positive authentically on social media is a different way of using social media than just scrolling through and comparing. When you put stuff out there for people to enjoy that is you making a choice to not waste your life and to move your life in a new and creative direction. The problem is when you sit around on your ass and compare your own miserable life with that of everybody else's. Mark

Twain said: "Comparison is the death of joy". And I couldn't agree more. Stop comparing your job to your friend's job. Stop comparing your love life to that of some random acquaintance. Stop comparing bodies. Make something of your life and find your own dreams. I promise you this. If you decide to get off your ass and make every day count, you will grow and enjoy life a little more every day.

REASON FOR DISCONTENT #2:
You are spoiled AS FUCK.

When I say that you are spoiled as fuck, I actually mean WE are ALL spoiled as fuck! It's time for a reality check. I am sorry to break it to you, but it's time for me to paint to you a picture of the harsh reality of living in the 21st century. I am guessing that if you are reading this you live in one of the wealthiest nations in the world. Today, when you woke up, I am guessing you were in a bed. Maybe even a California King with expensive sheets and a beautifully decorated bedroom. And I am almost positive that if you are reading this, you have Internet access, most likely on your phone. Your smartphone! Americans have become the most spoiled creatures on the planet. We have been blessed by our forefathers with freedoms that surpassed even their wildest dreams. We have been blessed with a mostly good economy. And yet here we sit, enjoying a comfortable, plush lifestyle, which most of us have squandered away with debt and irresponsible decisions, and complain about the temperature of our lattes.

Ever wondered why all the women in the "good ole days" appeared so hard? Those pioneering women with bustled, floor-length skirts, leather boots and a neck that never saw the light of day, dirty hands from hours of factory work, and hips for childbearing. Often with a stone cold face standing next to 6 scowling toddlers all in knee-length pea coats. These women bore and raised 8-15 children with little to no medical assistance. They lost many pregnancies. They had no heated showers or baths. If they were lucky enough to own a tub, the whole family took their bath in the same water, father first. Beds were piles of grass or straw with a canopy to catch stray critters. They had dirt floors, no gas, no electricity or running water. Just imagine freezing your ass off in the dead of winter, walking to the outhouse in the middle of the night, bare-assing that COLD seat! So how were some of the most hard working, malnourished, cold, dead-tired, uncomfortable women so content?

There was nothing like the true grit of American women in the early days of our country: hunters, homemakers, factory workers and military nurses. Their primitive lifestyle wasn't an issue because they knew that the work of their hands and sacrifices of their hearts would mean something in the new world. It was a hard life with worthy causes: family, freedom, ownership and a legacy. What happened to American women between then and now? We started getting too comfortable and we forgot what's worth fighting for. All the things that were just supposed to be luxuries distracted us. We got so spoiled that we lost track and it has made us discontent and miserable.

It is time we all hit our spoiled, entitled, fat-asses with some perspective. When is the last time you were cold? Can you even remember the last time you had a cold shower? What about the last time you were hungry? Like physically, painfully hungry? Probably never! Instead of walking up and taking your emotional temperature every morning, deciding how you feel after your long hot bubble bath and warm coffee, decide what you are thankful for. Decide what positive thoughts you'll dwell on and don't act like a spoiled bitch because it's making you discontent.

It is not my intention to make you feel like shit with this reality check. But I want to try to help ALL of us regain some perspective on how truly blessed we are. I am sure NONE of us have had an easy life, but I promise you, if you remain grateful for all of these things that you DO have, you will never be discontent.

REASON FOR DISCONTENT #3:
You are easily offended.

You're driving through the neighborhood and you see a friend jogging. You wave, and she doesn't wave back. You're instantly offended! Your mind starts racing and by the time you have parked your car, you have worked yourself up. You're actually pissed now. You thought you guys were friends, but apparently not! There goes her invitation to BBQ on Saturday. Or maybe you don't get angry when you get offended, but you get pathetic and start questioning every interaction you've ever had with your friend. She must be mad at you because you didn't like her new selfie post on the interwebs. Suddenly, it's 10pm and you've spent hours and hours being offended and now you're miserable and discontent with life in general. Let's rewind for a second. What actually happened when your friend didn't wave back? Your perception: She was rude and she was deliberately not waving back. Reality: Her brother called; his wife died. She went for a run to clear her head. She had no idea you waved. All she could think about were her niece and nephew.

When we judge other people's actions and motives we only hurt ourselves. We take offense and ultimately ruin our impression of potential friends, partners, or business associates. Even worse, we are destroying relationships with our spouses, significant others and family. If your boyfriend says something that you find offensive, then instead of letting it ruin your evening, try to communicate your expectations, stop assuming that you know what he was thinking and then just let it go. It's not worth missing out on an amazing evening of orgasms and snuggles with him just because you feel like his offensive comments earned him the emotional punishment of frigidness and silence. Being offended and clinging to it like you're entitled to feel that way makes you dissatisfied in life and that's how a miserable cow is born.

The truth is that you have no idea WHY anybody is doing anything just from judging his or her actions. And rarely do people do anything just to piss you off. If someone wants to listen to loud music in his big fat truck with the windows down, then stop thinking it's to annoy you. He is probably just enjoying himself because it's a nice day and he loves music. If one of your friends posts a ridiculously pointed meme with "hashtag code" that you are absolutely positive was directed at you, stop assuming you know which direction it was aimed at because I can almost guarantee you that it wasn't aimed at you and you have no idea what that meme or quote means to the person who posted it. So stop getting offended by random actions. Of course, it's completely normal to have opinions regarding a person's actions or behavior (although you should probably just keep those opinions to yourself). However, if you are putting together a motivation in your mind as to WHY someone is doing anything, you are judging him or her. And that's when you start feeling offended and butthurt. If you are judging other's motives you will always be discontent so just let it go.

REASON FOR DISCONTENT #4:
You are bored AF.

When you woke up this morning, did you lie in bed asking yourself: "How do I feel about getting up today?" Did you take time to assess how you were feeling emotionally? Or did you spend 30 minutes checking social media on your phone? If the answer is yes to any of these, then you have too much time on your hands. And you are probably sort of bored with your life. You might not be the kind of person that jumps out of bed every morning, but the way you start the day says a lot about your life. I start my days with a cup of coffee, but I fuel my life with purpose. This is going to sound a little condescending, but bear with me. I feel like boredom can really be the breeding ground for bad behaviors. Have you ever met a REALLY, REALLY bad dog? You go to your friend's house, their ScoobyDOO comes barreling around the corner, tackles you, slobbers on you, knocks your kids over, eats the Thanksgiving turkey, tears up your couch, shits in the entryway, and ultimately ruins your evening? Well, the thing that any good dog trainer will tell you is that some of the worst dogs are the most intelligent dogs. Because these high-energy dogs were bred to be highly trained working dogs, they have the potential to do things that we can only imagine. But unfortunately, people don't understand how to work with these kinds of dogs. They need somewhere to direct their physical and mental energies or they will have very bad behavior. Once you train a great Dane properly, you will have a protector, defender, and trusted companion. Now, am I saying we are all big, dumb animals? No, but I am saying if you aren't directing your physical and mental energies in a healthy way, your worst behaviors will surface: gossiping, shit-talking, complaining, and fight picking. I always find it amazing that my female friends with the very least to do (i.e. no jobs) have the "most to say" about my life, especially when I didn't ask their opinion. Stay busy, my friends.

Whenever I catch myself finding frivolous things to bitch about I realize that I need to get back to working towards my own goals. That usually means trying new things, starting lessons, failing, getting back up, and trying again. That's how you get out of the rut of a boring life and find satisfaction.

The people you surround yourself with are important when it comes to how boring your life is. If you spend most of your time with other miserable cows, then you will eventually get bored because a life of complaining and nagging isn't very stimulating. I'm grateful that my partner is one of the least boring men I have ever met and he has challenged me to get off my ass. The biggest thing I was drawn to when I met Nick was that he was super cause-oriented and had a passion for people and a passion for getting people the tools to get better – but more about that later.

HOW TO BE SUCCESSFUL: **Focus on your own shit.** Most likely the #1 reason you are discontent is because you have not found your passion, your mission or set new goals for yourself. You are afraid of change. I watch people settle every single day because they can't handle their fears of failure. You almost prefer the boring life because at least you won't have to challenge yourself. But if you want to be happy, you need to fight the comfortable, set goals, pursue your passion, make a plan and cultivate the life you really want.

REASON FOR DISCONTENT #5:

You are creatively insecure.

Last, but not least, of reasons for discontentment is creative insecurity. This one is my very favorite. Why? Because I believe over the years I have struggled with this one the most. If you find the corners of your mouth curling when you see the incredible accomplishments of your friends... If you notice a scrunch in your forehead when people are dishing out compliments to your spouse... If you hear critical thoughts pouring out of your mouth before you even realize you are speaking out loud. Your discontentment has overtaken you. And most likely, creative insecurity is the culprit. We've all seen it, people who are highly critical of others, putting others down, making known their dissatisfaction through the intolerance of others and the way they do things. Perhaps they are feeling shitty about themselves?

I spent my time in high school in a video production suite. I was editing videos and running around with a camera. I graduated film school at 20 years old with the aspirations of making movies. Shortly after, I got married, moved back home and spent the next four years pissing my time away at internships for random production companies and doing family photo shoots in the park. There is NOTHING wrong with that life. But I quickly realized that I was in a rut and I stopped creating. I simply wasn't challenging myself and I was afraid of doing anything new and interesting.

Meanwhile, with the launch of much cheaper DSLR cameras and social media like Pinterest, EVERY SINGLE girl I went to high school with became a "photographer" overnight. Over the next few months I watched their portfolios unfold and I spent a copious amount of time criticizing their work, talking shit about their cheap equipment, over-saturated filters, and awkward shot composition and poking fun at them on social media (MySpace). "Natural-Light Photography" just meant they didn't know how to operate studio lighting equipment or bounce boards. I had spent years going to trade shows and building a business and these girls just popped up out of nowhere and were teaching photography workshops. I was critical, rude and intolerant. Angered because I spent all my time and a lot of money on film school, and these girls didn't know the first thing about what they were doing, picked up a hobby and made it look like a business in no time. I was thoroughly discontent. And then it hit me, I was spewing negativity... meanwhile, what WAS I doing that was so great? I hadn't done anything new in months. I hadn't put out anything original or beautiful. I was in a rut, and I hadn't moved forward because of my own creative insecurities. I took a huge slice of humble pie and forced myself to go "LIKE" and "COMMENT" one nice thing to each of the photographers' work. I might not have liked it, but there was something positive to say about each of them. Then, it was back to the drawing board for me. Time to further develop my skill set.

Miserable cows are swiss-cheesed with insecurities. I think mine came from all the issues I was having in my marriage and my personal life. I forgot that I needed to keep growing. A degree from film school would only get me so far. It wasn't the end of my creative journey. The successful amateur photographers out there reminded me of that and I didn't like it at the time. But it was an eye-opener. Don't let insecurities stop your creative journey. You don't have to start out with a perfect product. Instead, develop a skillset. Every day we are faced with decisions. Decisions to be bitter or free. Decisions to stay in a rut or start creating again. Decisions to be a miserable cow or enjoy life. Let it go. The only person who is missing out on life and creativity is you.

DISCONTENTMENT IS A STATE OF MIND

If you want to live life to the fullest, demolishing your goals, surpassing your greatest expectations, you'll have to change the way you think. First of all, you need to realize that discontentment is a state of mind. To break the cycle of discontentment, you need to stop comparing, stop acting like a spoiled brat, stop getting offended so easily, get out of your boring everyday life, kick your creative insecurities and, most importantly, quit taking your emotional temperature every second of the day.

The truth is, your feelings are not the most important thing on earth. These days, most adults walk around with a poopy diaper; hypersensitive, overly emotional, letting the slightest feeling of discomfort become a foghorn start for bitching and complaining.

Emotions are a very important part of being human. Without them, we are basically robots. Feelings of pleasure move us closer to one another in relationships, while feelings of displeasure can keep us from reliving painful experiences. Without our body's physical response (rapid heartbeat, adrenaline rush) to an emotion of fear, we might not be capable of getting ourselves or loved ones out of harm's way in a life-threatening situation. The sociologist Peggy Thoits, who has spent her life researching society's idea of emotions, describes emotions as having many elements: emotions are a mix of physiological components, cultural labels, expressive body actions, and appraisal of situations and contexts. Webster's definition of emotions is a "natural instinctive state of mind deriving from one's circumstances, mood, or relationships with others." The fact that emotions are a state of mind means that they are always subject to change. We have all seen the feelings chart that shows all the different emotions. We typically use them as a tool to help children identify their feelings. And while it's very useful to be aware of your feelings, I truly believe we have placed all too much significance on feelings.

We've all heard stories of individuals being overcome with irrational fear because of past traumas or circumstances that trigger a physical response in their bodies. They can be physically comfortable and completely safe, but they are experiencing panic, stress and anxiety. Panic attacks, phobias, self-mutilation or suicide may seem extreme. For people who experience these emotions they are EXTREMELY real. Almost everyone I've known with severe depression struggles with it regardless of their current circumstances. This reminds us all that emotions truly are a state of mind, sometimes working independently of your current life circumstances. That's why a lot of miserable cows feel discontent even if they look like they have a very satisfying life from the outside.

As I mentioned before, emotions are a state of mind derived from our mood.

And our mood is usually directly related to our thoughts about our life and our circumstances. Just think about the situation of two siblings, raised in the same household, who wake up every morning under the same roof, with the same privilege, raised by the same parents, but Billy wakes up every morning with a chip on his shoulder in a miserable existence and Dillon wakes up reeling at the thought of all of the opportunities for adventure. How do these two seemingly mirror images of each other have such different outlooks. Well, it's because emotions are a choice. The physical responses we endure are a direct response to our emotions. Our emotions are guided by our thoughts. Therefore, if you can choose what you think about, you can choose how you feel. You can choose to get off your ass and think about your opportunities. You can focus on cultivating a great life instead of focusing on how miserable and discontent you are.

If you want to feel better, you need to get your head out of your ass. And if you are feeling like you might be a miserable cow who is succumbing to the culture of discontent, then here are some questions to ask yourself right now:

Are you mad at your significant other before they even come home from work?

Are you mad at your children before they even come home from school?

What about your friends? Do you believe they will always disappoint you?

Is nothing ever good enough for you?

Are you bored and at the same time holding yourself back from challenges?

Do you ever feel truly satisfied with anyone's efforts? What about your own efforts?

Do you feel cheated?

Do you feel alone or like people don't want to be around you?

Just as misery loves company, every miserable thought will be accompanied by yet another. You need to realize that you need to get away from the culture of discontentment and you need to choose a different state of mind every single day. It is possible to rewire your brain, to establish new thought patters, and to ultimately change your perception of the world.

CHAPTER 3

Love Is Not Possession

Iceland 2017 #mylove

I wrote this poem when I was in my early 20s:

Bright lights, new people, large moving machines.

Big stuffed animals, pink fluffy clouds, something from her dreams.

Dust on her sandals but she doesn't care.

Her mama put purple bows in her hair.

Everyone is laughing and smiles are really big.

Songs are getting louder… her brother dances a jig.

Her little heart is pumping more with every step

So much about this night she hopes she won't forget

The longest line she sees is the one for red balloons.

The thing she always wanted and never quite pursued.

She turns her big green eyes to daddy; he knows just what she wants.

Not even a word is spoken immediate response.

She waits and waits and waits in line for this new treat.

Tied to her hand, perfect apple red, looks good enough to eat.

All she can think about the rest of the night…

Protecting her new possession… impending fright!

I love my balloon; it is all that I desire

A night full of excitement, only IT lit my fire!

Clenching so tightly to the little white string...
All of these people, not sure what they'll bring.

Each element proposes feelings of eminent doom.
"Even wind could take my perfect, red balloon!"

Fear swallows her once excited, childish heart.
Anxiety fills her up, every single part.

"I must find a way to keep my precious gift
NEVER, NEVER, NEVER, I cannot ever let it drift"

Little hands climb up the string to pull it in her lap
Hugging it tightly to her chest her arms a little trap.

"I don't ever want to lose you, you mean so much to me.
You're mine forever and ever, I cannot set you free."

With each twinge of fear her grip gets a little tighter.
No space between the two, suddenly something bites her...

A big loud noise, POP... her love affair is shattered.

SHE LOST HER RED BALLOON, THE ONLY THING THAT MATTERED!

Her daddy picks her up, "Baby, I'm so sorry that happened!"
Tears roll down her rosy cheeks, she is oh-so saddened

"Daddy, I just didn't want to lose it… I loved it so very much!"
"Baby I must tell you something you may not fully touch…

The wind is not your enemy, it's fear that you should hate.
It's the one that stole your fun, the joy it would create.

Let's get one more balloon but this time keep in mind,
Enjoying every moment is your only job this time."

This might seem like a childish poem, but it was so close to what I was feeling and it helped me process some of the things I was going through. We protect the things we want and desire. We fear to leave them vulnerable so much that we can suffocate and harm them. Trying to control our circumstances, our life or our relationships is like trying to protect a balloon from popping. Relationships can be temporary and fleeting. Happiness comes and goes.

Sometimes the very best thing you can do with your life is to just enjoy the people in your life for the time that they are in it. Taking care of one another is important. The problem often arises when you try to cling to something. You become possessive and you run the risk of hurting the person or the thing you love and lose the joy of each moment.

If you're often feeling possessive of the people you love or if someone you love isn't giving you the space you need to cultivate the life you want, then that becomes a source of misery in your life. Miserable cows usually suffer from the misguided idea that love is a possession. These women maybe find a man that they like and once they are in a committed relationship, they get possessive and they lose the interest of the man of their dreams because he feels like he is being suffocated. Or sometimes, the miserable cow has been the victim of a man that feels like he owns her. Soon, she doesn't recognize herself anymore because she has changed so much and lost touch with her own goals and dreams in return for a relationship with a possessive man. The analogy goes both ways.

I've had my challenges when it comes to love. I was married twice and had to go through some dark stuff before I really realized that love is not possession. Finding a healthy partner is the most important choice you will ever make. Your spouse/life partner often will determine how far you go in life. Are you with someone who believes in you and encourages you to live your dreams? Do you encourage your partner to life their dreams? Does your partner let you be yourself? Or do you feel like you are suffocating each other in a miserable relationship where nobody is happy.

#GypsySoul

At the end of my first marriage, I came to the realization that I wasn't with someone who was "in love" with me, but more the idea of me. It made me furious. He was critical of me and of the way I did everything. The way he treated me was hurtful and ended up draining me of creative energy and joy. Just imagine going through every single day and the person you are supposed to trust and love is mentally pushing you down. I couldn't do anything right in his eyes. I couldn't even add a dish to the dishwasher properly. These little, everyday criticisms wore me down until I didn't even know what I wanted in life. I didn't even see how bad his abuse had become because I wasn't myself anymore after years of being miserable.

One episode stands out more than anything else from those many unhappy years. I remember I woke up one night, sick as a dog. I was careful and quiet so as not to wake him. He probably heard me, but he didn't move a muscle. After 6 hours of hacking my guts up over the porcelain throne, I was dehydrated, shaking and a little emotional. I finally lay back down in bed just as the sun was coming up and I got some sleep. Suddenly, I felt something wet and cold smack against my cheeks. And then I felt it again. I was woken up by my face being pounded with wet socks. Wet laundry thrown at me piece by piece from a soaked bag of wet clothes from across the room. "You like that?" he screamed at me, "Do you? I told you to put my clothes in the dryer, you idiot! What the fuck is wrong with you!" I don't even know how I was alright with that sort of behavior. I wish I could say the thirty-something me had some empathy for being treated that way. But I don't. I should have chosen better for myself. But this was typical stuff that went on another three years. He was always disgusted, disapproving and critical. And I allowed him to be. I was obviously not cultivating a life of happiness in this relationship. I had my work and I had a place to live. And I wasn't alone. That seemed like enough for me to stay with this man. This marriage was terrible and anybody can see that. But it's not always so simple. You might not wake up with wet laundry being thrown in your face after you've been up sick all night. You might just be in a mediocre relationship, but as the years drag on, it's drained you for energy and happiness. Maybe you meet disapproval when you bring up an exciting new work opportunity. Maybe your partner thinks it's a waste of money when you want to start a new and invigorating hobby. Or maybe he is always critical of the way you dress/eat/cook/talk. It doesn't matter. Over the years, it will drain you and you will be headed down the path to becoming a miserable cow. As time went on there weren't many fights that didn't end up with me getting thrown against a wall choked or chased through the house to be tripped or backhanded in the face basically just for existing in his world. One of our last fights ended with him kicking me into a wall that broke a mirror, and then him dragging me through shattered glass. When I was writing this I remembered what started the fight. I came home and woke him up from a nap with tickles. I was literally tickling him and it pissed him off. I didn't stop on command and he launched me into a wall. Because I was crying he got angrier and wanted to drag me out of the room to shut me up. He pulled my by my ankles through broken glass. I bled through my clothes and had to pull glass shards out of my sides. It is very hard not to become angry with myself for subjecting myself to such nonsense.

When I finally decided to leave him I sat him down at Chipotle and asked a series of questions. I think I already knew the answers to these, but for some reason I just needed to hear the answers so that I could gain some closure.

Me: "Why do you love me?"

Him: "Are you serious with this shit?"

Me: "Yes, please just give me a few reasons. I need to know."

I think at this point he mumbled something about my looks and added a "You're kind." at the end.

Me: "Why me, why do you want me? You always seem so upset and frustrated with me?"

He started to lose it, his faces was boiling.

Him: "Ali, I don't know what the fuck you're driving at here. Does it matter why…? I can have anyone I want. I chose you, so be happy about it."

At that point, it was not even surprising that he had reacted this way. When I asked him why he loved me, he didn't even know what to say. He didn't. However, it was clear from his last comment that he "wanted me", that he could "have anybody", and that he "chose me". He was treating me like his possession. He thought of me, and my love, as something that he owned and didn't have to work for or treasure. Rather than thinking of our marriage as a relationship between two independent individuals, he figured that love was a possession and that he could treat me however he wanted to.

I can't really hold this behavior against him. We were 19 when we married. He came from an abusive childhood. He barely knew me. How could he? He barely knew himself. The harsh reality is one I learned to understand much later. I was using him as well. I wanted to feel needed. I wanted to feel safe. I wanted to have my life figured out. I wanted to tie everything up and put a big red bow on it. I really don't believe it was even love. I was 19 and I wanted to be in control of my life. I wanted the next thing in life and it seemed like it was marriage. The thing about thinking of love as possession is that it is scary. Like the little girl with the red balloon, we are filled with anxiety when we think about losing someone's love. We want to tie it down and be sure that we have it forever. And that's why so many people end up in unhealthy relationships. They once experienced love for the other person, or at least the idea of the other person, and once married, they feel like they need to hold on to the relationship in order to hold on to love in their life. I have watched it happen, time and time again. Women wanting to be married so badly, that they don't care to whom. They just want love, safety, and commitment. They dive into any relationship and want to change their partner into something he isn't. Love is not possession. Love is finding a person you value, a person you have a connection with and choosing to cultivate something real, something lasting. Love is letting the person you fell in love with be exactly who they are. Love is not controlling, it's not jealous or vain. Real love is finding someone who looks out for your best interests. Don't you want to be with someone who actually DESIRES you? Desires to spend time with you?

If you are acting miserable, you are not desirable to anyone.

10.15.11 Wedding #2

I married my second husband because I was a damn wreck and he was nice to me. Really nice. I fell in love with his three little boys and I wanted to start a family. I spent the next 7 years raising kids. But this husband and I didn't have IT. I think we were together because we needed each other in the beginning. To this date, I can say that divorcing my second husband was the saddest and hardest thing I have ever done. Despite his depression, and his isolation, he was a very good man. And he was very good to me. He adored me, but he hated himself. He was so very stuck. For the 7 years we spent together I felt like I had a weight of heaviness around my neck and I was never able to make forward progress. His emotional struggles carried over to our boys and they struggled deeply as well. We both had shit to deal with. I would never blame him exclusively for what happened. But he had no life outside of me and he wanted to possess me completely. He spent a lot of his time trying to hide me from everyone else, always afraid someone would take me away. I felt like I couldn't breathe. I poured my heart and soul into his boys. But I did not have the affections to do the same for him. I'm sure that the reality was that he had an unquenchable thirst for more of me because I didn't want to be his. I was always keeping him at a distance because even though I loved and cared for him as a person, I had become his caretaker. I used to listen in bed when he would wake up and talk to himself in the bathroom mirror. He told himself every morning that he was a worthless piece of shit. That he was disgusting and trash. I could hear him whispering poisonous words to himself over the running water of the shower. I've never understood fully the burden that he carried. I'm not sure he did either. I spent years waking him up to nothing short of a circus performance to keep him from breaking down in tears. I always had to be ON because he was always miserable. I was exhausted. I never felt like he was the right person for me. I do not see our time together as a mistake, but as a chapter of my life. We were not right for each other. But that doesn't make it any less sad.

My first husband had no problem holding me back and he didn't want what was best for me. He thought he owned me and that made him treat me like shit. His power over me gave him a confidence boost. He was broken in his own way and our marriage was definitely broken. My second husband wanted me so badly that he ended up holding me back as well. He wanted to possess me so that I would never leave him. In the end, both relationships went wrong because we both treated love as possession and it made us miserable.

Let's get back to the miserable cow problem again. We probably all know the saying "Why buy the cow when you can get the milk for free?" This isn't a perfect metaphor for love, but stay with me for a moment here. So in this scenario, I'm the cow, my partner is a dairy consumer and he is supposed to buy me in order to receive my goods? And if I choose to give him my milk, I mean goods, before he makes the purchase then he might not ever purchase me? Which leads me to the question, who is he purchasing me from? My father? Is my father a dairy farmer? And why am I a cow...? If are talking about my father and potential partner, why aren't we all the same species? And... Why am I for sale? This metaphor has so many holes in it it's fucking exhausting and I'm going off topic here. But the truth is that old ladies used this metaphor for decades in order to get their granddaughters to realize the power of their "goods" when trying to get married. Call me a romantic, but I like to fall in love with someone who likes me for who I am and not for my potential milk stock that I won't dish out without a wedding band on my finger. In some countries, people are still bartered into arranged marriages. Our species was seemingly perpetuated by the original "Let's Make a Deal"-kind of love. Four cows, two goats, one plot of land and you have yourself a wife. Make babies, build families, work fields and repeat for generations.

In this country (and many others) marriage used to be a business transaction and somewhere along the line it became a meal ticket. Your husband might not have owned you, but you were pretty damn dependent on him. And like the cows he kept on the field, your husband was very dependent on you, too. You were worth something in terms of work and child rearing. One of the biggest problems with society today is a dysfunctional expectation of marriage. Instead of a bond of unity and family where husband and wife depended deeply on each other, it has become something so abstract that we don't know what to do with it. In bad situations, marriage becomes a symbol of ownership and possession. If your husband is emotionally broken, or if you are, then you start to think of love as a possession and marriage is the ultimate way to own your partner. You need to step back from that and choose to think of marriage as a union of love and commitment where you each have space and support to grow.

Finding a healthy partner is the most important choice you will ever make. Your spouse/life partner often will determine how far you go in life. Are you with someone who believes in you and encourages you to live your dreams? Do you encourage your partner to live their dreams? Does your partner let you be yourself? These are important questions and if you can't answer them honestly, then there is no way for you to move forward.

As mentioned, I was a wedding photographer and videographer for a years and years. I saw many crazy relationships in and out of my studio. It was honestly better than reality TV sometimes. I always joked around with my close girlfriends because I found something quite comical about how terrible some of these relationships were giving that these people were getting married. And while divorce isn't comical, I just couldn't help but laugh at the drama that indicated a future divorce. After a bitter divorce and lots of broken relationships, I felt entitled to my vantage point. I probably shouldn't have stayed in the wedding industry so long. Regardless, I found myself capturing hundreds of stories of newlyweds on their biggest day and I started placing mental bets on the couples I thought would make it. Usually I was right and even though sometimes I wasn't, I can honestly say many of those couples had no business being married. How did I place my bet? The moment the wedding became about the party instead of the celebration of the couple, I knew the bride and groom were headed for a bad marriage. If the bride was on the dance floor getting shit canned with her bridesmaids and grinding on her friends from high school... If the groom was MIA, taking shots in the back of the church during the first dance... In short, if the couple didn't even want to spend their wedding day together, I knew that they likely didn't have the right attitude to find things they would enjoy about and with each other in the 30 years to come. I understand that life is FULL of distractions. We all have something we could be doing. But if you can't find and keep interest in your mate on the day of your wedding, then don't get married. Your spouse is supposed to be the person that you enjoy above all others because it will be the person by your side for the rest of your life. You and your spouse are better off if you have a deep interest in each other and if you enjoy spending time together. And if you are willing to give each other the freedom to cultivate awesome lives together and apart.

My own stories tell you as much as the divorce statistics of the 21st century. The unhappy newlyweds go on to become unhappy married couples and at some point they hopefully realize their misery and choose to either work on their problems or get divorced. Inside the lives of unhappy married couples we find more miserable cows than I want to imagine. So many men choke out the creativity and beauty of their wives and turn them into miserable cows. The husband's own insecurities surface and eventually cause them to abuse and control his wife on some level or another. He becomes fearful that the world might see the incredible and fascinating things his spouse has inside. The thought of sharing her infuriates him so much that he takes her away so she can spend her life hiding them from the world, barefoot and pregnant in front of a stove. In the meantime, this puts cold emotional distance between them, which turns her into a tortured soul and a miserable cow. And of course he is afraid of losing her. He is treating her like shit. He doesn't offer her much. Just enough to keep her around. But not enough to make her flourish. In the end, he will look at his wife and wonder what it was that he fell in love with in the first place because he doesn't recognize this miserable cow that he has turned her into.

I'm not saying men are the only problem-makers in marriage. Women have their own way of controlling their husbands and treating them like possessions. Women, bitter, angry and entitled, will often end up destroying what's left of any early connection by trying to tame a wild thing. The man that they fell for slowly disappears as she tries to change him and control him in even the smallest matters. And he lets her because he loves her and wants to make her happy. You will see her demanding that her partner dress, talk and behave a certain way. This creates a destructive power struggle where two people are constantly fighting for control while trying to protect their own interests at all times. I am sorry, my friends, but love's not possession. The idea that you sign a document and suddenly you have control over another person's choices is preposterous. Our society needs to stop telling people that this is how marriage works. Marriage is not what it used to be. It needs to be a way to move forward together and not a way to stall your spouse or stop them from pursuing new goals and challenges.

The thing is, if you are going into a relationship because of what you think another person can do for you, you will **NEVER** be satisfied. You will become a miserable cow because you rely on someone else to do the hard work. Honestly, marriage isn't for everyone. But if you want to share your life with one person for as long as you both shall live, I urge you to consider this: Are you able to be your own person first? If you aren't sure what that means, then you aren't ready to be in a relationships. How can you grow as a couple if you don't even know how to grow as an individual? You will end up stuck in a negative spiral of complaining, nagging, controlling and being bored with your life. So figure your own stuff out. And the same goes for your partner. Encourage your mate to be his own person as well. The strongest relationships I've ever witnessed are between couples that have taken time to enjoy things in their lives apart from each other.

Now that I have talked about some of the issues that characterize the miserable cow, I think it's time to move forward. Even if you recognize every single problem I have covered, even if you are the most miserable of cows, you have a choice to change. I spent too many years feeling miserable, sorry for myself and angry at my circumstances.

It's a waste of life. Forgive, let go, move forward, enjoy the journey and cultivate the life you want. In the next few chapters, I'm going to talk about how to do this and how far I've come in my own life.

CHAPTER 4

Through the Fire

Strokkur Geysir #Iceland2017

"Listen for the lyrics that life wants to write with you." - unknown

We all have a story to tell. Maybe even a song to write. I read this quote today and it inspired me.

In my painful past, in the hardest times of my life, I remember waking up and feeling very alone. I remember feeling like nothing would ever change. I used to lie on the floor and beg God for something to change. Now I see, I had the ability to make that change. Even though I didn't feel like it at the time. Those times were only a part of the song. The slow part of the song in the beginning before the chorus or the key change or even a chord progression.

There are many very important lessons that we learn through the hardest times in our lives. That is IF we actually decide to walk through the fire. It will always be easier to numb the pain. In fact I spent a good portion of my life "numbing the pain" But if we choose to let ourselves grieve, deepen our perspective, and burn, really burn in the darkest hours of our lives, we will come out stronger than before. The key is to face your inner demons and work on your mental attitude.

10 years after my first divorce, I find myself looking back at everything; at lives I built and destroyed. My first husband called me about a year ago to apologize for our traumatic relationship. He didn't want anything from me.

He didn't request my forgiveness. For the first time on his own personal journey, he recognized his personal pain had ruthlessly gutted me from the inside and he wanted me to know that he was sorry. He told me he loved me and that if he could have done it all again he only wished he would have been more self-aware and gotten the help he needed before he was responsible for hurting anyone else. I thought I was completely past everything. But I found myself pouring my heart out and telling him how all the things he had done to me had been so destructive. After an hour on the phone I think we both had forgiven each other and I was truly able to let all of it go.

I met the love of my life 4 years ago. I am sure it wasn't the best time for either of us to be in a relationship. But the compatibility and connection pushed us together like a great storm. The hardest part about our relationship seemed to be the baggage we both carried from our pasts. For the first time in my life I am with a man who is with me, not because he needs me, but because he deeply loves me. We have a vision and passion for life that surpasses anything I've ever experienced. We've traveled the world together. We've built businesses together and personally urged one another to grow and surpass our greatest expectations. EVERYONE who has ever seen the two of us in action has the very same reaction. "MAN! You two are perfect for each other." From our morning coffee and goal writing, to the way we can work a room. Each of us with our own goals and creative ideas, it seems there is no one that can stand in our way. No one besides ourselves.

Nick is a Special Operations Marine Raider. He served in the military at the height of our generation's war on terror. His life is a bleeding example of perseverance through adversity. He blew past every statistic for a youth of his age and circumstance and poured himself into service to live a life of service and dedication to his country. I remember listening to radio interviews he had done before I met him, utterly blown away by such a young man with so much determination and perspective. He was well traveled, smart, and eloquent. He entered a room with such a presence that others looked to him for leadership. He could surf and rock-climb. He loved movies and production. He was creative and compassionate. He even had a motorcycle! My gypsy spirit couldn't resist this kind of person.

Nick spent the first 5 years after his military service working on himself. I have never seen a more proactive approach to emotional health or a better mental attitude.

But Nick, like so many men in our generation, spent his young adulthood at war. I will never fully grasp the things he went through; the heaviness he felt losing his brothers or the weight he has on his heart for every veteran who made it home so very different. When we first met, Nick liked to sleep alone. He works hard and doesn't quit. Nick doesn't like to be around sniveling victims. He is a hard-nosed achiever with very little empathy for anyone who isn't working towards bettering his or her life. His goals are clear. The path to get there is clear, and if you are in his way then you might get trampled. All the things I love about Nick are the same things that I can take personally and experience sensitivity to. At times, I have to remind myself of what amazing things we can do together. For the first time in my life I am with the person who encourages me to achieve my goals, forces me to push myself past the point of pain and work harder. Just like my second husband used to hide me from the world, Nick wants to share me with the world.

Surf City. 2015 #RideorDie

Meeting Nick was not the solution to all my problems. I have more personal fears and insecurities than I would like to admit. I can never actually remember a time in my life when I was insecure or jealous in a romantic relationship until I met Nick. The beginning of our time together was very wild and messy. Neither of us was looking out for the best interest of well… anyone. And Nick did a lot of things that hurt me. On top of that, the pain from my past lurks around dark corners at times and it seems that I alone am in charge of instigating every blow-out and grounding our plane every time we take flight. How can it be that for the first time when I find myself with the man of my dreams, in the life I've always wanted, that I am still struggling with my old problems as well as creating new ones? Why do I find myself looking for problems? Why does it seem at times that I may be sabotaging my own dreams? This comes back to some of the things I've already talked about – you have to work on yourself before you can be happy and be in a healthy relationship. So even after I met Nick, things were not perfect. I found myself ultimately becoming the very thing that I have always hated; the thing that my mother taught me not to be; the thing that I find most disgusting in the world - I was becoming a miserable cow. I thought I had left those days behind me, but I was wrong.

I found myself fixated on my partner and everything he was doing right or wrong. I was convinced he needed to be more how I WANTED him to be. Instead of investing in myself or my goals I was perturbed that he wasn't fulfilling my needs or giving me the things that I wanted, when I wanted them.

I gained weight. My health became the last of my concerns. I felt so insecure with myself that I started to lose sight of who I was. I became obsessed with my appearance. It didn't help that I was getting older and in every photo of me, I thought that I was covered with wrinkles and even grey hairs. I started to make it my mission to fix my face and my body artificially. First I got Botox treatments and lip injections, then filler in my smile lines, and finally I got my boobs done. Now there is nothing wrong with any of these things. In fact, I had wanted to get my boobs done for most of my life. But the problem was that I really believed that those things would somehow make me feel better. Somehow having my ideal appearance would make me feel like the woman I wanted to be. It couldn't have been further from the truth. I had built up having huge tits in my mind for so long. I really believed it would change things for me. 3 months after my boob job I had a meltdown in a dressing room. The thing no one tells you about fake tits is that they make you look fat, pretty much all the time, unless you're wearing skin-tight clothes. Nope, attempting to fix all the things I didn't like about my outward appearance did absolutely not make me happy. It left me more frustrated with myself if anything.

Next I tried my old strategy of not giving a shit. My thinking was that if I can pop pills or smoke weed and check out, I won't feel anything. I won't feel the frustration and the misery. Comfortably numb was an all-too-familiar feeling in those days. The problem with numb is that you can't truly hide from yourself and your feelings. Wherever you go or whatever you take… **there you are**. You can't ever get away from the person you're trying to escape. This phase was fortunately very short lived. It took me only a few months to realize that I had to deal, like REALLY deal, with the daunting notion that I WAS UNHAPPY because I was unhappy with myself.

Kansas City, MO #Crossroads

The reality is that your life can be amazing and you can have the perfect body, but your thinking can still hold you back and get you stuck in misery. We might all benefit from some serious therapy, but in the meantime, there is a surprising amount of work that you can do on your own.

Right now, you can sit down and decide to work on your mental attitude and I promise you that it will be worth it. The single most useful resource I came across is the work of Dr. David Burns. Now, stay with me because some of this might seem a little technical, but if you let it sink in and apply it to your own life, it's going to change you.

Dr. David Burns created a list of cognitive distortions, or mental misconceptions. His belief is that each of us has created distorted beliefs based on upsetting or traumatic events from our past. These cognitive distortions are extremely dangerous because there is a good chance you filter all of your thoughts, actions and beliefs through the pain of the traumatic or upsetting event, and you will ultimately be sabotaging your own happiness because of these distortions.

Here is **Dr. Burns' list of 10 cognitive distortions** and my hope is that, like myself, you can identify your negative thought-patterns and hopefully see an opportunity for growth and personal development so that you can break out of your misery:

DISTORTION #1: All or Nothing Thinking

You view things in absolute, black and white categories.

With this belief, this is a hard world to live in because it means that either you are perfect or you are a worthless piece of shit. For the miserable cow, this usually means something along the lines of not allowing yourself or other people to fall short of perfect. So when you look yourself in the mirror, you won't notice that you look like a healthy 30-year old women, but you will focus on the 2 gray hairs that have popped up overnight. And you start calling yourself an ugly old witch. Or maybe you had a great weekend with your spouse with lots of sex and new challenges together, but then he chooses a movie you don't want to watch on Sunday night and suddenly the weekend goes from "perfect" to "the worst". It can be hard to catch this sort of thinking if it's become part of your normal thinking, but if you find yourself measuring everything against an idea of perfect, you are probably caught in this distortion and you need to nuance your thinking. The world is not black and white, but shades of grey, so instead of telling yourself that you look like an ugly old witch, focus on the fact that we all have flaws and that it isn't worth getting upset about.

DISTORTION #2: Overgeneralization

You view a negative event as a never-ending pattern of defeat: "This always happens to me!"
We all have issues with this one because it can be hard to not see patterns in our lives. But if you use the words ALWAYS or NEVER a lot, then this is probably a big issue for you and it's holding you back in life. You have to eliminate those words from your vocabulary. Maybe have someone help you to get started with this. Or start with some of the really persistent thoughts such as "I'm NEVER going to be happy." Ask yourself if you are being truly honest with yourself. Weren't you actually pretty happy the other night when you were sharing some good food with your friends? Try to nuance your experiences and your life so that you don't feel trapped in unhappiness because of your need to be a drama queen and your need to overgeneralize things.

DISTORTION #3: Mental Filter

You dwell on negatives and ignore the positives.
The mental filter can affect your life in a really negative way. It's a little different from the other two distortions because you don't necessarily overgeneralize or put matters

into black-and-white categories, but you do become obsessively focused on either the negatives or the positives and forget the bigger picture. Maybe this looks like you only focusing on how your mother didn't like your cookies, but the rest of the family raved about them. And now all you can hear is your mom mumbling that pecans don't belong in chocolate chip cookies. Or maybe you get a really shitty comment on your latest YouTube video and you focus on that instead of the hundreds of positive comments. You filter the world through one negative element. How about you spend as much time on the negative as it deserves. Think about whether the negative can be used to improve yourself and if it can't then get over it. Let it go. It's not worth your time.

DISTORTION #4: Discounting the Positive

You insist that your positive qualities don't count. Imagine this: you've put on your new dress, you've done your makeup, and your spouse walks into the room and sees you standing there looking sexy as hell. He can't help but to tell you how sexy you are. But his comment falls flat to the ground because you tell him that you don't actually look great, in fact you look kind of fat, and you tell him this with a sour attitude. Just accept the compliment! He has a right to an opinion. And you might actually look really great. You don't have to trap yourself in misery by always putting yourself down. It's not good for you and it's not good for your relationship. Your man is going to get tired of you getting bitchy when he tells you that you look good so he is going to stop telling you. And you are going to resent him for never giving you compliments. But you probably did that to yourself by always discounting the positive. If you're not ready to actually accept the positive, then at least shut up and thank whoever says something positive.

DISTORTION #5: Jumping to Conclusions

You jump to conclusions not warranted by the facts. Jumping to conclusions can take the form of mind reading where you assume that people are reacting negatively to you. Or the form of fortune telling where you think you can predict that things will turn out badly. The issue of mind reading is almost self-explanatory. You assume that you know what people are thinking and even if you are assuming that they are thinking something positive about you, it's not really helpful. You need to let go of this habit and focus on how you want to behave and how you want to meet the world. Do you want to be a miserable cow or do you want to cultivate a happy life? If you want to be happy then stop jumping to conclusions. The same goes for the idea of fortune telling. You simply have no idea what is going to happen in your life. You might be experiencing the best day of your life tomorrow. Or the worst. You might be a couple of minutes from a major plot twist that will change your life forever. There is nothing useful in thinking you know what's going to happen in your life. If you keep insisting that nothing good will ever come to you, then no wonder you feel miserable because that's a really depressing, and completely wrong, thought.

DISTORTION #6: Magnification of Minimization

You blow things out of proportion or shrink them. It's obviously not ideal if you blow things out of proportions. You will find yourself overwhelmed and you won't be able to make positive changes. Or you overreact to little things and soon, you will find yourself friendless because nobody wants your drama. It's also a problem if you minimize important elements in your life. For example, if you tell yourself that it's not that big of a deal that you are waking up miserable every single day then you won't have the motivation to make the right changes. It's all about trying to see the situation for what it is. A trusted friend might be better at seeing things clearly because they aren't as close to them as you are. So if you are having problems figuring out if you are blowing things out of proportions or shrinking them too much, then ask an honest friend for a reality check.

DISTORTION #7: Emotional Reasoning

You reason from your FEELINGS: "I feel like my husband wants someone else so it must be true."
But the thing is... your feelings are not really worth trusting. They don't tell you what the situation is actually like. If you end up following your emotional reasoning you could be making terrible mistakes. Your husband might actually want you, but you find yourself arguing all the time and you are accusing him of cheating on you. That will hurt you and your relationships more than you can imagine. Ask yourself if your reasoning is built on reality or on your feelings. Better yet, ask yourself if you're about to start your period and go get a bottle of wine and some chocolate and chill the fuck out.

DISTORTION #8: Should Statements

You use shoulds, shouldn'ts, musts, or oughts, and have-tos. These words are a little bit like "always", "never", "perfect", "failure" – they are dangerous and if you catch yourself using them a lot, it's a sign that you are deep in the mess of distorted thinking. Miserable cows have a long list of "shoulds" and "shouldn'ts", but they never get any further. They will sit around and complain about their weight and how they "should get a gym membership" or "shouldn't go out to eat so often". Instead of using these words, decide to follow through. You clearly know how to solve your issue. It will make you feel better than complaining about your life to anybody and everybody. Ask yourself a more positive question. What do I need to do to make it to the gym 4 times this week? How can I make time for food prep? What are some ways to make some extra money each month to afford a baby sitter for more date nights? If you aren't going to follow through, then you are probably not motivated enough so let go of whatever idea you're clinging to. And follow your passions instead.

DISTORTION #9: Labeling

Instead of saying "I made a mistake," you say: "I'm a jerk" or "I'm a loser". If you wouldn't use a label about a dear friend, then you probably need to stop using it about yourself. When we label others around us: he's a womanizer or she's a liar… We are really saying, "this is who they are and it isn't going to change." When I left my first husband I always said the worst things about him to my mother. She loved him dearly and it pissed me off. I told her all the time he was a liar, and abuser, and a thief. I think my best label was that he was a "scam-artist." All these labels did was make it more challenging for ME to let go and forgive. When he called me to apologize last year, he told me over and over; "I didn't do anything right by you, I lied, I cheated you out of happiness, I used you." Every single thing he said was true and suddenly all the words I spoke over him lost their power. By apologizing he didn't only free himself, he freed me. I have to admit I felt like I was over it, like I didn't care anymore, but the phone call made me realize that I still needed to heal, I still needed to let go of my judgments. Using labels will lock you in, it will put others in a box. Even if they are positive.

You are too complicated to label. So just stop labeling yourself or other people and you will be surprised how much you can grow

Street Art #chickswhoclick

DISTORTION #10: Blame

You find fault instead of solving the problem.

This is the classic miserable cow bitch fest. It's not pretty to observe. Some people love blaming themselves for everything that has ever gone wrong and some people put all the blame on others and assume the victim role. If you start getting obsessive and blame yourself for things that weren't within your control, you'll break yourself down. It will be like carrying the weight of the world and that leaves any woman open to becoming a miserable cow because taking on that much blame will destroy you. On the other hand, if you are always blaming everybody else and acting like a victim, how are you ever going to change and take charge of your own happiness? It's a difficult balance, but like all the other cognitive distortions, we are looking for a way to separate misconceptions from reality.

So there it is, I read these and instantly realized my problem. It was like a light bulb came on. But it came on while I was holding an exposed electrical wire, soaking wet, and I was electrocuted with this information. Suddenly, it all made sense. I'm fucked up. My ideas of the world are fucked up. Sure, there are things that partners need from each other. But, being a miserable cow means being a bottomless pit of needs.

Nick had changed so dramatically from when we first met. He had chosen to face his mental misconceptions. The longer we were together, the closer we became (despite my bitchy tendencies) and we really developed a bond that changed. We went from "hanging out" and being a low-key couple that ran together to building a life with each other in a year and half. He had so many fears about relationships from his past. He wasn't ready to commit to me, or anyone, early on in our relationship. That really hurt - it made me feel vulnerable and insecure. I put up walls, I acted like I didn't give a shit and I started "doing my own thing." Ultimately, I was in pain. I CHOSE to filter those feelings through the heartbreak in my past and ultimately magnified his fears in my own mind. I took everything he said to heart. I convinced myself that I was with the wrong person and I was going to feel "TRAPPED" again with the wrong person. Suddenly, a fight about line sprints or lunges during a workout became a blowout about not feeling loved and I was threatening to move out. I was always threatening to move out. It was my go-to move. I leave. I am very good at leaving. A trash bag full of clothes in the back of my pick-up and this gypsy was off on a new "adventure". Somehow I idealized the lifestyle in my mind. A gypsy - hippie with nothing "holding me down" traveling the globe with messy wind-blown hair and not a care in my mind. I think I've actually made an Instagram post just like that one. Nothing could be further from the truth. The free-spirit girl that I strived to be throughout my 20s had turned out to be nothing more than a shell. My lifestyle was one of pain, loneliness, and debt collectors blowing up my phone 24/7… That was if I could keep my phone on that month. I so thoroughly despised the miserable cow that I thought the answer for me was to be alone, care-free and worldly. Now, don't get me wrong. I have had a lot of amazing adventures. I've always lived my life to the fullest and truly done my very best to enjoy the journey. But it isn't that black and white. What I am saying is that if you aren't getting what you want from your partner, you have to cultivate it with communication and love. Create happiness. No one is responsible for your happiness but YOU. And happiness often means changing your mental attitude and facing all your cognitive distortions and your mental misconceptions.

Life is hard. Life isn't fair. And I have realized that your attitude affects your outcome 100%. Little choices every single day gives you the happiness you are searching for. It was a long road for me to get to a place where I realized that this was the case. I had to admit that I was a mess. I had to admit I made bad decisions and that I wasn't a victim of my circumstance. I had to admit my insecurities and baggage were sabotaging my life and I had to decide that I wanted to be free. And now that I am here, I can promise you that getting your mental attitude under control is worth it. Write down a list of all those things you keep telling yourself. Listen to that inner voice that is constantly making you miserable. And question everything it's been saying. See if you can identify what kind of cognitive distortions you are dealing with. And then go through the fire to find a better mental attitude.

No matter what we want to think, life isn't fair. Life isn't kind or merciful. One of my good friends is going through a very difficult time. No, fuck that. One of my good friends lost her husband suddenly in a tragic accident and she is going through the most difficult time in her life. But she is motivated. Motivated to do all the things that would make him proud. Every day she wakes up with that sense of purpose. This week, I watched her emerge herself in the fire and I have never been more inspired in my life. Her courage is captivating. To anyone going through the darkness. Do not give up. There are incredible things waiting on the other side. Do not be afraid to feel. And do not be afraid to face yourself and your problems. Your inner demons are usually the most difficult to combat.

Back to Nick and I - Things had changed dramatically between us. He loved every part of who I was. He was trying so hard to build a life with me and I couldn't even see it because I was so miserable! It was time to KILL the cow, but I didn't know how to do so. What I've learned is that two things work better than anything: gratitude and forgiveness. So let's dive into those.

Gratitude #lotus

CHAPTER 5

The Lotus – Gratitude is Everything

"Gratitude unlocks the fullness of life. It turns what we have into enough, and more. It turns denial into acceptance, chaos to order, confusion to clarity. It can turn a meal into a feast, a house into a home, a stranger into a friend. Gratitude makes sense of our past, brings peace for today, and brings vision for tomorrow." - Melody Beattie

So working in the military space has introduced me to a term that captures the idea of a miserable cow almost perfectly: the dependapotamus. A dependapotamus is a "dependent", meaning the spouse of a service member. She is usually overweight, unhealthy, not very charming and miserable. She often ends up being a stay-at-home mom, but the truth is that she doesn't do a damn thing except sitting on the couch all day, enjoying all the benefits of her husband's hard work and leaching off the system.

These obnoxious, lazy, and immature women are the complete opposite of their spouses. They don't appreciate the life they have and they feel entitled to a great life, but are not willing to work for it. What's fascinating is that the dependapotamus' behavior carries into all walks of life and shows the classic miserable cow in action. These women have no real skillset and they are not interested in growing or developing themselves. They have kids, but they spend almost no time on them. Instead, they are consumed with their own misery and the whereabouts of their husbands. They know he might leave them because all they do is complain and nag. They are completely incapable of seeing how ungrateful they are. In fact, not a day goes by where the ungratefulness of the dependapotamus doesn't spew from her blow-hole. I know – I'm being harsh. But apparently this phenomenon is so wide spread that they have been given the title of "dependapotamus" and an urban dictionary definition on the interwebs. But listen, ladies, marriage is not a meal ticket. Just because you signed documents saying you share a last name doesn't mean you own a person. If you don't gain some self-respect and invest in your own life and your relationship, you'll lose his heart. And if you don't stop to think about all the things you have to be grateful for, you will stay on the pasture of miserable cows forever.

It is very easy to sit and pull apart the things that make us unhappy with our partner, without life and with our kids. He does this wrong. She can't get this right. They are too loud. Each of us has the opportunities daily to think about the things we are thankful for or to complain about the things we aren't. Especially moms need to think about this because it is truly a hard job to be a good mom and show up for your kids every single day.

I feel like I could write a book about raising stepkids. I spent 7 years raising boys. My second husband's children from a previous relationship. It was the most special experience I ever had in my life and I will forever be thankful to my second husband for giving me that opportunity. That being said, it was the hardest and most thankless job I've ever had. I met my boys when they were 3, 7 and 8 years old and I think I spent the first year doing nothing but snuggling them and playing freeze tag in the back yard with water guns. Their biological mother was scarcely around for those first four years we were married. She was going through her own painful journey, I'm sure. My second husband and I met and moved in together within three months of dating. His ex hadn't even signed the divorce papers yet. She left for a 19 year-old kid who lived in his mom's basement and she herself was homeless and living out of her van for quite some time. So I was a full time parent right from the start. Raising step kids is obviously quite different than the bond created from raising a baby from infancy, but those boys were my world. If you're in a situation like mine then you understand that the hardest part is sacrificing everything and realizing there will always be a hole in their heart for their biological parent. You cannot fill it. Their mom kept them at just enough of a distance for them to put her on a pedestal. She was the unattainable parent that they loved unconditionally. I was doing mountains of laundry, wiping snotty noses, packing lunches, checking homework and reading bedtime stories, yet they still spent many nights crying, missing their real mommy as I rubbed their heads to sleep. It was always hard for me. I love them with all my heart. There isn't a single day that I don't think about them. There isn't a single day that I don't wish I could spend sitting beside them, listening to them ramble about school, or Minecraft, or girls.

I learned a very valuable lesson raising my boys. Time just vanishes. Time flies. One day you're having day adventures going to the marble factory and the zoo. Countless hours in the park, jumping on the trampoline, water fights in the yard and nerf wars, oh the nerf wars. And then suddenly, you find yourself sending them a text to be home before midnight.

I cherished every moment with my boys. But I remember the exhausting things as well. I spent my summers nannying for three extra kiddos so that I could be at home with the boys. I was a real soccer mom with a minivan and everything. I remember one fall afternoon I had a breakdown. I had a house full of children climbing the walls (I say house but it was actually the size of an apartment). My youngest was home getting breathing treatments with a nebulizer every few hours, the nanny kids created a giant mud hole in my yard where they buried all of my sons' toys, and tracked mud all through the house. The 10-month old I was watching was covering my walls with peanut butter and jelly, the giant oversized cat, Moses, took a colossal shit in my bedroom and I stepped in it barefoot. I ran to the bathroom to wash my foot while stumbling on a Lego death trap along the way. I threw water on my face and sat on the edge of the tub to take a deep breath. I caught a glimpse of myself in the mirror and nearly fell backwards into the tub. I was a train wreck. Dirty hair, food on my face, and something I couldn't identify on my shirt. Just when I decided to fix myself, a pair of 4 year-old paws and an iPad slid themselves under the doorway. "CAN YOU PUT IN YOUR PASSWORD?" Sweet Jesus, I couldn't catch a minute and a half to myself. It was at this moment I started to laugh. It couldn't have been any more comical and I knew it.

My husband facetimed me and I was laughing hysterically at the irony of my lifestyle changes in such a short amount of time. In less than two years I went from lying awake in a cold, dark apartment with a bottle of whiskey to becoming Insta-mommy covered in baby food, cat shit... and children literally climbing the walls. I remember telling my second husband in bed one night that I felt like the boys were suffocating me. They followed me around the house like little ducks. The climbed on me, hung on me, they wanted to play 24/7. I told him I just needed like a night off. And then it happened... TIME FLEW. Suddenly, I was, standing in front of their bedroom doors like Anna from Frozen begging them to come and build a snowman in the front yard. You see, because I came in the picture when the boys were already older children, it was like they turned into teenagers overnight. They went from being my best little buddies and my grocery store sidekicks to giant, 6ft tall, carb-loading, teenagers. The older boys didn't want to play anymore. Well, not with me anyways. And I realized how fleeting that special time with my obnoxious monsters truly was. Time vanished. I never took another minute with my youngest for granted. When he asked if we could go to the park, the answer was always,

"Yes." When I started to overhear women complain about there fussy toddlers or their clingy 7 year-olds I would lose it. I felt it my duty to make sure none of my friends took the special moments with their kiddos for granted because they are only little for such a short amount of time. Moms, you have to take time to be grateful or you will waste the beauty of motherhood in exchange for misery.

Women have truly taken a back seat on their own personal development and growth. They use "stay-at-home-mom" as an excuse. I spent 7 years raising boys and I can honestly say, although I felt trapped in a suffocating marriage, I tried so hard to "be me" and to continue to work on myself . I cut out time wasters like TV and spent quality time with my boys AND quality time with my writing and art. No, I wasn't "furthering my career," but I was developing my brain and interests. Find out who it is you are again. Find out what you like to do. Pursue it. Passionately. Maybe your vision IS your family. Well, take time, write out your goals and make plans. If you can go back to school, develop a skillset - DO IT! If you can't afford it, try some online classes. Hell, watch a free online tutorial and try something new. I taught myself programs like Photoshop and Lightroom, even video editing software from online tutorials. Taking the time to develop yourself will release you from creative insecurity. And it will make you grateful for the life you are creating.

Gratitude is the only thing that will ever truly release you from misery. It is imperative that you understand there isn't a way that things are "supposed to be." The entitlement of our culture has led us to believe that if we work hard we will have what we want. Things don't always work out that way. But, if you work hard and commit you will get closer to your goals every day. With a positive mental attitude, no matter what happens in your life - death, divorces, affairs, abuse, foreclosures, bankruptcies - there is one thing they can't take away from you. And that is your personal development. Knowledge, wisdom, skills, education, insight, creativity. They aren't tangible and they can't be taken away. Unless someone literally drops a piano on your head.

I read the following words recently, and I think it reminds us all of the secret of happiness and work:

Emily's Lotus #artineverything

"Just as water cannot wet the lotus leaf, so work cannot bind the unselfish man by giving rise to attachment to results.... Even though the lotus is rooted in mud, it continues to float on the water without becoming wet or muddy. This aspect of the lotus dictates how humans ought to live in this world – work incessantly but be not attached to the work and to the surroundings." - **Swami Vivekanand**

Remember to serve this universe with gratitude. Don't be attached to the result. Be excited that you get to work on something and that you have the chance to cultivate a happy life. God, your friends, your family, your boss, the people you meet everyday - show them gratitude. The peace, bliss, and power that you seek all come from within. If you are a miserable cow, if you are a dependapotamus, if you are an unhappy mom, then you don't have to stay trapped in that way of thinking. You can sit down right now and make a list of all the things you are grateful for. And all the things you want to do – and then do them and feel the gratitude in your life crush all the misery and unhappiness.

Steven Aitchison famously said: *"Successful people have a sense of gratitude, unsuccessful people have a sense of entitlement."* Even if you are in the depth of motherhood with cat shit on your floors and children climbing your walls, life is about so much more than "SURVIVAL," it's about growth, it's about thriving! Don't act like you are helpless or powerless in your life. By definition, helplessness is the inability to defend oneself or to act effectively. Powerlessness is the belief that you have less ability to change your life than you actually do. Your mind is a powerful thing and your body is a powerful thing, but you have to train it. If you feel helpless and powerless, know that those are just beliefs that are keeping you stuck. Use all the great things in your life to cultivate gratitude and fight the negative emotions. If you feel insecure, take the time to develop yourself and you will inherit a new sense of confidence. **WHAT IS THE ONE THING THAT NO ONE ON EARTH CAN EVER TAKE AWAY FROM YOU?** Money comes and goes, people will abandon you, relationships end. I have lost homes, money, cars, marriages, friends... But the one thing that no one can ever take away from me is time and energy. I have spent so much time and energy developing a skillset, learning new things, internships, learning from the best, and educating myself in my field. **YOU ARE NOT A VICTIM.** If you see yourself as powerless, you will remain that way and it will always be someone else's fault.

There is hope. If you find yourself always leaning towards the negative, if you are constantly being critical of others, unthankful for their efforts, here's the truth: It's time to develop yourself. Negative, discontent people have one thing in common: too much time wasted on nothing. Rest and relaxation are necessary, but if you find yourself zoning out on junk TV, gossip magazines, and pinning EVERYONE ELSE'S good ideas, recipes and vacations, you might need to refocus your energies. Although Pinterest is a great concept, I truly believe it has become a way for bored, introverted housewives to live vicariously through the Internet. GO OUT AND LIVE LIFE. Make your OWN pins. Take your own adventures. Post your own memes. And for God's sake, tell your own stories!

Trust me, I realize that life can suck. Really bad. Although it doesn't have to. Nobody denies that life can weigh us down. The mind is often a deceitful friend. Thoughts can send you to another place - both good or bad. You can attempt to master your thoughts or let them rule you. Even if you try to control your thoughts, your mind will infiltrate your dreams and your attitude will shape your life. Just remember you're loved. And you have something to love. Give thanks. Hold your loved ones tight. Rock that minivan life! Call your granny and tell her you love her, listen to her stories. Thank your spouse for his hard work. Gratitude is the only way to stop being a miserable cow. If you embrace a grateful attitude, you will finally be able to develop yourself and work towards your something by focusing on creating something, loving something, or supporting something. Set goals, smash them. Live life. Focus on your own shit. Enjoy the ride. And be grateful for all that you have.

I truly believe that thanksgiving is the cure. Only with gratitude can we heal the cells from the inside out. It is perfectly impossible to be thankful and complain at the same time. Gratitude and thoughts of thankfulness can actually change your neuro-pathways, creating cellular change in your brain. Change the way you speak and you'll change the way you live. GIVE YOURSELF A BRAIN DETOX! Spend the next 7 days sharing what you are most thankful for! The simple act of sharing will change your perception and feelings on your current situation. Positive mental attitude will attract positive outcomes in your life TODAY.

CHAPTER 6

Forgiveness – Letting Go

Mom and Pops #mymakers

As I said earlier, using labels will lock you in. Even if they are positive. You are too complicated to label. So just let go of labeling yourself or other people and you will be surprised how much you can grow

There was a time I woke up every morning excited about life and everything that MIGHT happen that day. Like a little kid packing his backpack full of things to take on his next big adventure. Each new day meant possibilities and that was thrilling for me. All I ever wanted was EVERYTHING. Travel, friends, family, experiences! That didn't last very long…

In the midst of your misery, you might ask yourself: "what happened to me?" The answer is never that complicated. Life happened. You grew up and you got a taste of what the real world is like. You end up screwing yourself over by making bad choices. Or you experience more disappointments, pain and heartbreak than you had ever expected. You're probably telling yourself that no one understands what you are going through. You've probably isolated yourself from people who care about you. You're holding on to all this hurt and it's slowly killing you. You are probably angry with yourself, your family, your exes… the world in general. And you don't even recognize that excited young woman that you used to be.

Generally, women hold on to the anger and the hurt from the men in their lives. You feel like your ex is the reason why you are miserable. You are absolutely certain that he was the one that messed up your life. You wake up in the morning feeling like a reflection of your former self. Maybe he cheated just that one time. Or maybe he had an affair. Maybe he betrayed you with someone very close to you. Maybe he stole the best years of your life and tore your heart out. Maybe he hit you. Maybe he trapped you in the house, chased you from room to room and pulled your hair out, slammed you into walls, broke mirrors and pictures, choked you, and dragged you through the glass on the floor because you woke him up from a nap.

There is no doubt that my first husband mistreated me. There is no doubt that he was an unstable individual who ruined sex for me for years. But guess what, **it was not about me.**

In this life, I have been abused, mistreated, cheated on, and seemingly had my heart ripped from my chest. And in this life I myself have cheated, ruined relationships, broken up families, and left a path of destruction in my wake. And guess what, it wasn't about them.

Hurting people HURT people, and that's the bottom line. The selfish choices we make affect everyone.
I truly believe that the inability to forgive is the number one reason people are afflicted with ulcers, cancer, and just

about every other terminal illness. Emotions play a huge role in our physical bodies. The way we process or refuse to process our emotions - the way we cope, or refuse to cope - can eat away at us from the inside out. We have ALL done wrong to someone in our lives. I can say personally, over the years I have probably hurt just as many people as I have helped. Forgiving yourself is step one. Letting go of your past, releasing yourself from your mistakes and wrong-doings. If you can't forgive yourself, your past will haunt you forever. Next, we have to forgive others. It won't happen overnight. Pain and suffering are not your friends. Each day you spend playing things over and over again in your head, will destroy you. You will always be a captive in the prison of your own mind, until you forgive, let go and move forward. Jonathan Houie said: *"Forgive others not because they deserve forgiveness, but because you deserve peace."*

So this is the chapter where you decide if you are ready to let the pain of your past go. If you are willing to give up your misery. If you are willing to stop labeling others and yourself for past mistakes. If you aren't ready to forgive yourself, or others then you've reached the end of the line. Forgiveness is the first step to forward movement.

If you decide to keep reading, I hope these next pages can help you to release what you are holding on to, towards yourself or someone else.

Slow Dancing in a #BurningRoom

COLLECTING BAGGAGE

The story I am about to tell you is one that I have never told anyone. The only person who knows it is the person whom I am speaking about and for the sake of privacy we will call him Bo.

I started working with a much older man when I was married to my first husband. Things were horrible at home and just the idea of this guy swinging by my office was all I needed to get through the day. He was fascinating and comfortable all at the same time. Bo was a musician as well as a businessman. Every thought in his brain kept me engaged. I would typically see him every other day. He found reasons to swing by my studio as often as possible. He finally asked for my number. We spent every spare moment talking about life and peeling back layers to a "beautiful disaster". For the first time in my life I felt like I had met my match. And then it hit me. I was crazy about him. This person I had never touched, never kissed, never even seen outside of work was all I thought about. Bo was married. Bo lived at home with his wife. I was also married. I also lived at home with my husband. Bo traveled regularly for work and could call me freely. I guess we felt like we weren't cheating because we weren't sleeping together. I think I justified everything in my own mind by convincing myself I deserved to feel good. One night I snuck out of my bedroom to drive around the neighborhood and talk to Bo while he was on one of his work trips. We stayed on the phone for 7 hours that night. We never ran out of things to talk about. I came home in the morning and my husband didn't even notice I had been out. I knew something had to give. I couldn't carry on like that anymore. The night I left my first husband "after the Chipotle incident" was one of the worst. Bo called and I snatched my phone off the counter a little too quickly. My husband realized something was up. We spent the next 4 hours physically fighting and screaming. He took all of the keys, chased me through bedrooms and slammed me into walls, tackling me to the ground. I remember flailing underneath him pleading with him to let me go. All he wanted was access to all of my emails and Facebook messages. My heart was pounding. I remember screaming so loud that my head hurt. My face was soaked in tears, it felt like he was spitting when he choked me against walls and screamed in my face. I remember thinking if I didn't get out of the house that night, I might not make it out of the house ever again. Finally, he called my mom to try to get her on his side. She realized through my hysteria that I was in danger. She told him he had to give me my car keys. He told her he would only let me leave if I opened all my social media and messaging accounts. My mom, scared for my safety, told me to open all the accounts and leave immediately. So that is exactly what I did. I drove to my best friend's house right away. As absolutely exhausting and intense as that night had been, I remember hugging her so hard and smiling. I was free. She lied next to me and stroked my head. She told me over and over that everything was going to be ok, I was free.

Things could have been ok. But things were not ok. It is not an excuse, but as a 23 year-old I am not sure I had the emotional intelligence to handle anything that was happening in my life. Bo left his wife and children and the two of us carried on a relationship in private for 2 more years. The very, very sad reality was that the two of us were giving each other what we wanted and needed at the time and we were too selfish to care how our actions affected anyone else. Bo was tortured inside - living without his kids was destroying him. The guilt of his choices was eating away at him. He developed a drinking problem to cope. Then he finally made a decision that he could no longer live with what he had done and he decided it was time to go back. His wife was a very good woman who never gave up on him. But Bo and I continued back and forth communications for some time thereafter. I never fully understood the gravity of the situation. Until one day, his wife messaged me. She did not attack me, she did not call me names, she was respectful. She told me how much pain I had inflicted on her and her family and pleaded with me to stop posting things on social media to get his attention. She explained how hard she was trying to keep her family together despite everything that had happened, and very graciously asked me to stop. I remember I gasped for air after reading it. How could this woman be so vulnerable with me? She knew her husband was still checking my social media and she was asking me as a woman to understand and stop. To this day I am blown away by the dignity and composure of this woman and I will feel in debt to her for the rest of my life. The pain I caused her will never be excused, but the truth is that my selfish actions and personal destruction haunted me for years to come. I have also been cheated on and lied to. Used. By the person I loved most in the world. I know what it feels like to inflict that kind of pain on another person. I would like to say that was the last mistake like that I ever made. But it wasn't. I made more just like that one. I hurt more people. I spent a decade punishing myself and my body, living in my own misery. I went down dark roads in my twenties. I spent most nights working as late as possible and finishing the night with as much alcohol or as many party drugs as I could get my hands on. I partied myself destitute. I watched as an entire generation around me did the same. I was underweight and unhealthy. It became a joke amongst my friends. If you can't find Ali... check the shower. Most parties ended with me naked in a stranger's shower, covered in my own vomit. I got drunk enough to keep myself from standing upright. When the room started to spin, I would get naked and pass out in a hot shower. I am not really sure what ended up being the straw that broke the camel's back. I remember waking up at a boyfriend's house after a coke bender and feeling like I had been beat with a baseball bat, everything hurt and I had nothing. I knew something had to change but I didn't know how.

You see, the only thing that could truly free me from my past was for me to find a place for forgiveness. I had to forgive my first husband for hurting me. I had to forgive myself for being an ugly human. And I had to release it and move forward with my life.

I know there are hundreds of people with much worse stories than me. Ones with pain that wasn't so self-inflicted. People who truly are victims to their life's circumstances. And maybe that is you. Maybe you are the person with the absolute worst-case scenario of them all. As you read this, you think, that little home-wrecker "she doesn't understand MY circumstance". Or maybe you are the woman whose husband left her for 23-year-old me. And you can't live with that. Please remember that you don't have to. I would never suggest that someone stay in a harmful and unhealthy relationship. But no matter the circumstance, if you want true freedom, happiness and joy in your life, you'll have to forgive and let-go of the pain from your past to release yourself from misery. *"Forgive others not because they deserve forgiveness, but because you deserve peace."*

I cleaned up my act, got re-married. Raised children (did a damn good job). Devoted my life to family. Spent the remainder of my twenties trying to build a business and figure out who I was. There were good times and bad. All-in-all I believe raising children is truly how I learned to be a better person.

STEP #1: Forgiving yourself

As I said before, I have hurt so many people in my life. It can be painful to face that truth. Most of them, I didn't intend to hurt to be honest, but some of them I did. If you look closely, you'll probably find that the same is true in your life. You might not have had an affair or been abusive, but you have probably done little things that truly hurt someone.

In order for you to move forward with your life, you need to face all this pain you've caused. When my first husband called me to apologize, I realized that it must have taken a lot for him to face what he did to me. But he needed to do that in order to become a happier and healthier person. Hiding your ugly past will not make it go away. People talk so much about "embracing the struggle." How about let's just start with FACING it. I think he needed to reach out. But you might not need to. You might just have to look yourself in the eye and tell yourself that you are ready to forgive yourself for all the shit you have done. And that includes all the shit you have done to yourself. You might never actually feel better, but at least you are in the process of dealing with these things and you are not letting them weigh you down in the same way as they used to. Letting go of your past mistakes and forgiving yourself is definitely step #1 in cultivating a happier life.

STEP #2: Forgiving others

The next step, I think, is to start forgiving the people in your life who have hurt you. For me, letting go of the anger and resentment towards my first husband set me free. A gypsy can't live tied down by the past or by the mistakes other people have made. So I made an effort to free myself of that pain.

A lot of what I have dealt with has been pretty serious. An abusive relationship. That's not something you just forgive. But I think it's important to not make this about the big issues only. It's also about all the little stuff that nags you every single day. It's easy enough to forgive your husband for not kissing you goodbye in the morning once. But after 10 years together and him forgetting to do it hundreds of times, that anger starts to build up. And it destroys your relationship little by little. You need to work on forgiving the big stuff and the little stuff. You need to stop keeping score. You need to stop living in the past. Take control of the present instead and let others know your boundaries and your expectations. You'll be much happier that way.

Life is Tight #Letitbe

STEP #3: Let go and let life happen

The last step is much more spiritual. It's all about forgiving the universe/God/life for everything it has and hasn't done to you. I believe in creating your own life, but I also know that life throws you some curve balls from time to time. And if you don't watch out, you'll get stuck obsessing about those things. You had a plan. You had a goal. You worked hard. And then something you couldn't control happened and it seems like everything in your life fell apart. You felt entitled to things turning out a certain way and now you're holding on to anger towards life. It's not worth it. In fact, there are two things in this life of which I am quite certain:

1. The path you think that you are taking will most likely not lead you to your final destination.

2. If it does, it might not be exactly where you wanted to go.

In my early twenties I read a story that helped me process life as I knew it. It was called *"Birds. Letting Life Happen."* Now, I don't remember the author, or exactly how it went. But I do remember, that the idea was that if you spend your time trying to catch a bird, your hands will be constantly grasping, reaching and closed. And if you spend your time on your tippy toes, reaching for something that was meant to be free and trying to bring it into captivity, you could very well miss much of the precious time you have on earth. If, however, you simply stand still and calm, enjoying the grass at your feet, the cool breeze, and the path you are taking... perhaps the bird will land on you in her own time. The story impacted me greatly. So much, in fact... I got a tattoo of birds traveling around my arm to remind me to LET LIFE HAPPEN. Does this mean to sit around and do nothing? Absolutely not. But what it does mean is that each and every person should spend less time trying to control the circumstances around them, and more time enjoying the journey. You need to forgive the universe/life/God for all the stuff that has happened to you. All the shitty circumstances. If you do this, if you let go of feeling entitled to a specific way of life, then you can truly start living your life.

STOP trying to force your life forward. As my mom always said: "You can't squeeze blood from a turnip." No matter how hard you try, there will be certain people in your life that can truly only give you JUST that... a special time in your life. There will be people who you can love. But only love so far. There will be jobs and things you do, that you can only do for a season. You will GROW past people, friends, and even family. This is all part of the journey.

I encourage you only to live in the present, enjoy the journey, break away from what you cannot change. Let the world do what it needs to do. Don't hold any anger towards it. Be grateful for the experiences you have had, and remember: WORK HARD and LET LIFE HAPPEN.

The idea that at some point you will "ARRIVE" in your perfect home with white picket fence and 3.5 children. It's all going to be perfect, right? Granite countertops? Absolutely. A handsome husband? You bet! You almost feel like everybody, especially you, deserves this dream life. If you have even just the smallest voice inside your head telling you this, then you need to take a deep breath and let go. You need to just forgive the universe/God/life for not being perfect and not living up to your standards.

I had a brilliant childhood with loving parents. I am 33 years old. In my short life I have been married and divorced twice, raised 3 children, and moved 18 times since I turned 18. The past 14 years of adulthood I believe I have been waiting for some sort of "bliss" to arrive. I worked my ass off for it. I spent my early twenties working 70 hours a week... just to survive. Thinking that if only I got all the puzzle pieces to fit just right, if I did the right things and helped the right people, at some point life would get easier. Well, as everyone knows, it doesn't always get easier. Some days are easier than others. Some weeks are more enjoyable than the ones before it, but the idea that at some point the stars will align and fairytales come true will leave you very bitter in the long run. People will disappoint you. Friends, husbands, parents - they are just people. Here is what I've learned: YOU'VE GOT TO ENJOY THE JOURNEY. Live in the present. Suddenly your eyes will light up to all the special little things you've been missing. But you have to just let life happen for this happiness to come along.

There was a time I was trying to forge a path through rock, on my very own, without a drill. Just climbing and ripping through rock with my bare hands and all alone. It was messy, painful, but most of all... futile. It was Jim Watkins that said: *"A river cuts through rock not because of its power, but its persistence."* You see, "LET IT BE" doesn't mean I am encouraging you to "give up" on life, or become helpless. I am telling you that if you PERSIST in life, WORK hard, ENJOY the journey, focus on being GRATEFUL and ditch the entitlement, then your path will cut through rock effortlessly… well, almost.

CHAPTER 7

How to Kill A Cow

Iceland Adventures #unstoppable

There is more than one way to skin a cat. There are many ways to skin a cat. During my junior year in anatomy class I learned all the amazing ways to skin a cat. My cat Jezebelle lied there reeking of formaldehyde as I pulled her skin off with a scalpel. Some people cut the skin off. Not me. I pulled it right off and separated each bit from the fascia. Don't judge me. It was actually a fascinating experience. Anyways, back on track, there were many ways to skin a cat just like there are many ways to kill a cow. I think the best way to kill an animal of that magnitude is quickly, so they don't feel anything. They say that if you take too long, and the animal feels threatened, the stress hormones ruin the meat. So it's always best to just go about the morning like everything is normal and then, well, take them out. Although, in reality you might find that taking care of your miserable cow tendencies takes a lot of time. And you also may find that you revert back to your miserable cow ways under times of stress and pressure. The most important thing is that you become self-aware. You can identify when you are becoming bitter, nagging, or discontent, and you are able to deal with your attitude before it spreads and leads you back to distorted thought patterns and bad behaviors.

So how do I recommend killing your inner miserable cow? Well, first you should address the 6 traits of a miserable cow: your resting bitch face, your conversational soft kill, your nagging, your complaining, your jealousy, and your entitlement. Identify which ones you are struggling with. And honesty is really key in this phase. The next step is to think about why you are so discontent in your life. Why do you have all these miserable cow tendencies? You can go back and read about all these reasons in chapter 2, but again, I think you need to sit down and address these reasons one by one. It won't be pretty, but growth usually isn't. The third step I would recommend would be to think about your relationships. Are you feeling entitled to the love you're given? Are you acting like a possessive maniac? Is your significant other? Are you encouraging each other to grow or are you holding each other back? Our relationships carry so much weight when it comes to how we feel about our lives. Miserable relationships will eventually turn you into a miserable cow. So make a decision to work on the way you love. We all know that this requires a change in attitude so if you want to look at some ways to combat your distorted thinking, check out chapter 4 with a list of Dr. Burns' 10 cognitive distortions. They changed my life in such a massive way. They got me to look at myself more honestly and that allowed me to move forward.

When you've addressed all these unpleasant elements in your life and you are left thinking – what's up with all the negativity? You are ready to move on. Focus on two elements in your life: gratitude and forgiveness. You can read about those in chapters 5 and 6. I truly believe that you can handle life much better if you forgive yourself and others for what has happened in the past. And I think that gratitude is absolutely necessary if you want to cultivate a happy life.

But now, for the final step, I have listed 7 ways to kill a cow. I needed to kill mine in order to live out my free-spirit, artistic gypsy dreams and start cultivating a life of love, happiness, creativity, and adventure. Make choices that work for YOU. Leave your past behind and embrace what's in front of you. It's never too late to start living life to the fullest. Don't give up. And don't be a miserable cow!

#1. REWIRE YOUR BRAIN

Grab the biggest knife you can find in your drawer and charge at the miserable cow by rewiring your brain! You need to start asking yourself these questions: How can I become a more happy and positive person? What time am I wasting during the day that I could be applying to personal development? What thoughts can I dwell on that will help me feel more positive about my circumstances? What am I thankful for? The reality is that if you are looking for ways to be more positive, more thankful, and more empowered, you will find them! To truly understand the power that your mind has over your will and actions you have to understand the way that your brain works. When you have a thought, it creates an emotion (positive or negative); this means it has moved into your conscious mind and creates a signal and your hypothalamus responds to that signal. That signal creates a physical response in the rest of your body. Your brain starts releasing chemicals like serotonin and glutamate and eventually begins to create a memory. So just like that your thought created an emotion, a physical response, and a lasting memory. When you are stressed or anxious your pituitary gland OVER-produces these chemicals. The result is chaotic or cloudy thinking. You aren't even thinking clearly under stress. Next, your endocrine system takes over with fight or flight. Suddenly your normal healthy process of critical thinking has turned off and you are now in survival mode. Pretty much the opposite is true when you are fueling yourself with positive emotions. Even very difficult situations will get translated in your brain into memories of overcoming challenges or being a badass if that's how you're thinking about them.

Your thoughts are so much more important than the circumstances you find yourself in. So don't feel like it's a good idea to always be pessimistic. That's not going to get you anywhere. Look for the positive and you will experience how your whole body starts reacting differently to life.

So how do you reject negative thoughts? You protect what you put into your brain. You need to REJECT the stressful, negative, overwhelming, compulsive SHIT that tries to creep on your brain. Maybe you will have to change the things you do during the day. Maybe you will have to eliminate negative people from your life. Stop checking your man's phone 24/7. Stop looking for ways to catch him in a lie. It's not worth pursuing unhappiness. You will end up so stuck in that way of thinking that every second of every day becomes a stressful and anxiety-filled nightmare. I know that all you are trying to do is protect yourself from getting hurt by being paranoid and negative. But what you end up doing is hurting yourself without any real life reason. Do you see how pointless that is?

So start focusing your attention on your goals, hopes and dreams instead. If someone comes to you with an earful of drama, it's time to say

"MISS ME WITH THE BULLSHIT." Nobody's got time for that. The most important part of being successful is focusing on your own shit. Stop letting negative influences infiltrate your thought patterns and your attitude. I don't think I hate anything more than listening to women bitch about their husbands and kids. The same women who wanted so badly to get married that they set ultimatums for their boyfriends, rushed into getting a family started, and brokered their current relationship status. They want their husband to make more money so they push him to take the desk job and then complain that he works too much. They wanted to have kids so badly and now that they are 8 year-olds swinging from the rafters and they want to complain that they have too much on their plate. Seriously, ladies. Do you see the irony?

It is so important that you put some perspective on your thought life. Never take for granted the people you have in your life. Treat every day as a gift. REWIRE your brain by telling yourself how thankful you are for everything and everyone you have. Choose positive things to think about. Eliminate negative influences. Speaking positive affirmations over yourself is an exceptional way to start. So for a start, practice these declarations:

Today, I am grateful. I am healthy, content and hopeful. I am hardworking, strong and full of purpose and intent. My hard work speaks for itself.

My future is bright and I am constantly filled with new creative ideas. Every day is an opportunity for new adventures.

If you are as serious about this as I think you are, I highly recommend the book *"Switch on Your Brain: The Key to Peak Happiness, Thinking, and Health"* by Dr. Caroline Leaf. It walks you through a 21-day brain detox. If you are going to make some real progress with personal development, this book is a must! Some people have described it as an owner's manual for how our brains work, and that's basically what it is. And who can't afford to do a 21-day experiment in the grand scheme of things? It is our happiness that's on the line after all.

Greece 2016 #enjoythejourney

#2. BE PRESENT

The next attack on the miserable cow can best be described in the words of Thich Nhat Hanh: *"If we are not fully ourselves, truly in the present moment, we miss everything."* I am going to ask you to consider the following very carefully:

Have you ever wondered if you are truly present in every moment? For a large part of my life I've felt like I am watching a screenplay of my own life... present only for personal, thought provoking commentary behind the scenes (in my head). Maybe that is why I make a pretty good photographer. I still remember the first time I heard the term "fly on the wall" referring to photojournalism. It sounded just right. I can stick myself in the mix of someone else's party, event, wedding and watch their moments behind layers of glass. Don't get me wrong; I love my job behind the scenes. But the more I think about it, I don't want to miss everything. I don't want to miss my own life. I want to live VIBRANTLY in every moment. Maybe you're an introvert, or a thinker. Sometimes it's hard for a "thinker" to keep herself fully involved in every situation of life. Experiencing all of the good stuff. Finding the place, the person, with whom you "fit."

I believe as the years go by, we can get so caught up in the day-to-day... The mundane, the chores, the cat videos, the social media. We forget to be connected with our lives, our relationships, and our heart. We walk around disconnected from the life we are living. Maybe because it's a miserable life. But in order for you to crush that misery, you need to start connecting and feeling all the ups and downs of life. So here are three ways to be more actively present in your daily life:

A. TAKE PHONE BREAKS

Obviously we all have to work and most of us do our work on our phone these days. I literally run about 7 different social media accounts on about 10 different platforms. I use my phone for EVERYTHING. However, when it's time to connect with your partner, your kids or even yourself... Leave your phone in another room. I try to give myself full breaks away from my phone to listen to my own thoughts. It is amazing how many good ideas that start to flow when I open up my mind to creative thought.

B. EAT MEALS AT THE TABLE

I don't know what happened that made families move dinner from the table to the couch, but I HATE it! Nick and I have always believed that there is something almost spiritual about sharing a meal with friends and family. A glass of wine, a delicious meal and a simple "How was your day?" can open the evening up to endless relationship possibilities. It's in the real conversations about one another's day that we can pick up on the things going on in our kids' lives, our partner's life or our friends' lives. This is the kind of stuff that you CANNOT pick up through a text message.

C. LOOK 'EM IN THE EYE

People communicate more with their eyes than even words. They truly are windows to our souls. We find it easier or maybe just less intrusive to look away when people are talking. Maybe it makes us feel less vulnerable. But there is no better way to communicate insignificance to the people in our lives than to look away when they are speaking. Letting ourselves become distracted when we need to be engaged will ruin friendships and ultimately remove us from the present.

So I challenge you, as I challenge myself. Don't forget to connect with your life, your art, your music, your writing, your heart, your little people, your friends, your people. Take the time to listen, watch, and enjoy. What do you want to do more than anything else? One life. That's all we've got. Don't miss everything.

#3. GET HEALTHY

Feeling a little insecure about your body? Welcome to the fucking club. I was a boisterous 11-year old covered with freckles, and the proud owner of a pair of braces and random head gear. To top it all off, I was stuffed into a private-school uniform like a butterball in rubber bag. I always had body image issues. I struggled with anorexic tendencies all through junior high and in high school. It wasn't that I wanted to be perfect. I just wanted to look like Liv Tyler on the movie poster for Empire Records. I will never look like teenage Liv Tyler. I probably won't ever look like a fitness model, although I will likely never stop trying to attain that goal if I'm completely honest. But beauty is fleeting. Attain your ideal image and you will always find more flaws.

One of my co-workers put on weight a few years back. Enough that she felt uncomfortable in her own skin. I would ask her to go out and do things and she never wanted to leave the house. She was miserable. How can we as women choose to miss out on life because of our outward appearance? There is something wrong with our culture for putting so much pressure on women's looks. It leaves us miserable. There is always going to be something wrong with the way you look if your goal is to look like Liv Tyler on a movie poster. Even Liv Tyler doesn't look like Liv Tyler on a movie poster. Long story short, I felt terrible for my friend for how insecure she was feeling and what she was going through. It also made me think about my own physical goals in life.

Rhode Island #BFF

My fitness goal has always and will always be to be able to physically participate in living life to the fullest. Hiking, climbing, swimming, biking. whatever it may be. Count me in. I can guarantee you that if you are feeling insecure about your outward appearance it is affecting every decision you make. This takes the focus away from the need to look like a model and makes you think about what you want to do with your body. And for me, I just want to live life to the fullest. I don't want to be so out of shape that I can't take a hiking trip with my significant other. I don't want to be so overweight that I can't play nerf wars with the kids. My body is an important tool for cultivating the life I want. And luckily, I don't have to look like Liv Tyler in order to be able to go on a great hike or take a fun snowboarding lesson. In other news, I definitely DON'T look like a young Liv Tyler when I am crashing my ass down the bunny slopes (in case you were wondering), but I am living my life to the fullest!

I am positive that if are lying around on your sofa, pinning workouts on Pinterest, complaining to your spouse that you can't fit into your clothes… then you are miserable cow. You can't sit around and be miserable and upset that you don't have the body that you want if you don't work for it. You are NOT entitled to a great body, but you can work for one. My first piece of advice is to stop eating shit! Garbage in, garbage out. Just about anything that negatively affects your body can be cured with proper nutrition. I am NOT a nutritionist. But I can tell you one thing. If you live in the United States then you consume TOO DAMN MUCH. Turning to food as a comfort, or making food a reward will destroy your progress. I suggest downloading the MyFitnessPal App on your phone and keeping track of what you put in your body. Just tracking your calories alone can be an eye opener. Also, don't get sucked into thinking that there is some magical supplement that is going to make you feel better and lose weight. If you are eating shit, drinking too much, and sitting on the couch most of the day, then there is no supplement or fad diet that will actually help you. You need to get on top of the basics first. And that means eating some healthy foods. I'm not saying you have to down three kale smoothies every morning, but maybe start eating eggs or oatmeal for breakfast instead of sugary cereal or Pop-Tarts. Add some fruit and vegetables to your plate. Drink a lot of water. Get some good protein. This really isn't rocket science so don't be intimidated. It's like everything else in life: every day you are presented with endless opportunities to make a good choice or a bad choice. Try to make good choices most of the time on most days, and you will start to feel better soon.

My second piece of advice is to start exercising. Exercise is the most effective way to improve your mood and mental health. Studies have shown that those who exercise regularly beat depression, anxiety, ADHD, and MAD COW DISEASE (ok, not that last one). But crushing it in the gym will relieve stress, improve memory, help you sleep better and boost overall mood. And it might make you fit into your old clothes again. If you're making excuses for why you can't exercise then you are convincing yourself you can't change. Ask yourself HOW you can make time for the gym. Write down your fitness goals. Stare at the ass you want. Think about all the fun you can have when you start to move better. Sometimes when I am on the verge of an actual meltdown and everything in the entire world feels like it's going to explode, if I can just get my ass on a bike… in 55 minutes I will feel like a different person. The best way to get over break-ups, get past pain, and work through relentless disappointment is to challenge yourself with a physical goal. The overall sense of accomplishment will take you to new levels of confidence. I often find that when I am working out regularly, I FEEL like I look much better than I actually do. And that's what it's all about, baby! If you can't make it to the gym every day, then I'm sure there is some other way you can exercise: go for a walk, find a yoga video on YouTube, do 100 burpees, play with your kids for an hour. Again, it doesn't have to be so complicated, but it will make a big difference in your life.

Once you have a better baseline for your health by not eating shit and by exercising, you will find yourself feeling nothing like a heifer anymore. It will be like you dropped this heavy weight mentally and emotionally. This won't happen overnight, but it will creep up on you. Your body will be happy and ready to get you to where you want to be in life. You won't have to waste energy making excuses for yourself because you are doing what you need to do. Your significant other will start looking at you differently, not just because you look sexy as hell, but because you have stopped being this whiney and complaining couch cow. You will be able to go explore the world with him. You will be able to buy the clothes you like. So get off your ass! Throw out that box of Pop-Tarts! Get a gym buddy and a new pair of workout tops. Maybe it's as simple as you talking to a specialist about getting your hormones on track, naturally. Coming off of harmful drugs that affect your levels can change everything. Many people don't know it, but anti-depressants and pain pills will destroy your sexual appetite and your energy levels. Literally everything we need to be a happy and healthy individual is within us. Get with a professional and find out what areas you are struggling in. It's time to move towards a happier life.

Adventures of Ali #chickswhoclick

#4. DEVELOP A SKILLSET

This book definitely wasn't intended to give you a warm and fuzzy. No, I grasp that you probably won't feel great after reading parts of it. Even writing it, I have challenged myself to face all my demons, look my fears dead in the eye, and come to complete skin-crawling vulnerability so that I might accomplish one thing. IF I am so lucky to accomplish this ONE thing, then I will feel as though my mission was complete. This book was not intended to hurt feelings. But I am sure that it will. My mission was solely to create a really unsettled feeling inside the pit of your stomach. Something that won't go away. Something that you can't stop thinking about until you get off your ass and make a plan. A plan to change your life, your attitude, your relationships and your mind. If you take only one thing away from all of this clamor than I pray it be this ONE bullet: **you need to develop a skillset!**

For centuries women have put themselves in a position subordinate to men. Like the youngest child, screaming to be heard, accepted, and included. Women have spoiled their rightful place with spitting, fighting demands to be praised, adored and treated as "equals". Fourth-wave feminists have actually only accelerated this very disgusting behavior by losing sight of their true value and worth. Somewhere along the line we lost sight of what it truly means to be a woman. NEWSFLASH -Men and women are different. There will ALWAYS be some sexist jackass with a tiny dick that wants to treat women like objects.

THAT is not YOUR problem. Do you want to be treated better? Exude confidence. Worry less about proving yourself or your worth. Step into the strength and beauty of your true identity. A lioness doesn't throw a tantrum when her mate won't listen to her qualms. No, the female lion is too busy being a badass and hunting for her tribe. Antelopes, buffalo, impalas, zebras, wild hogs, and wildebeest - she doesn't have time to bitch about her place in the ranks. Female lions work together to bring down their prey.

What would our culture be like if men and women saw each other as powerful units and not as a threat. If we could see each other as "mankind" instead of fighting for gender rights to be heard and esteemed, how much would we accomplish? We would be a more powerful society than others around us. The Greeks had a vision for a powerful family unit such as this. Even in their art and architecture, women were depicted as strong, hearty fighters and beautiful vessels of strength. Warriors would leave to fight battles in complete confidence because the women they left behind were physically fit, educated strategists trained to fight and protect their families.

So many women have broken through the unique challenges that come from being a female in this world. If you are finding yourself feeling like you aren't able to do anything and that developing a skillset is never going to change anything, then try to find a female role model in your life. Someone that is so inspiring that you can only get to work on your own personal trip. I have found much inspiration in the Queen of Soul, Aretha Franklin, who recently passed away. One of her famous quotes is: "Be your own artist, and always be confident in what you're doing. If you're not confident, you might as well not be doing it." I think that one of the reasons this quote speaks to strongly to me is that it speaks about the creative insecurity that I have struggled with most of my life. Aretha Franklin tells us to pursue art and to do it with all the confidence we can muster. Even if you don't feel very confident right now, you can always try to find something you've accomplished in the past to feel good about, maybe it has to do with your dedication to your pursuit of happiness, or maybe it's plain old "fake it till you make it"-confidence. Stop trying to find confidence in other people's reactions to you and find your own confidence. You deserve to be your own artist, whatever that looks like.

It's time to see yourself differently! The very best way to see yourself as a strong, capable and valuable member of society is to actually become just that. It truly makes me sad that I see so many women in my own generation giving up on their own hopes and dreams because of creative insecurity or a lack of self-worth.

I would venture to guess that if you are unhappy, if you are constantly dissatisfied with your relationships, preoccupied with your spouse, then you are unhappy and dissatisfied with yourself on a very deep level. If you pull your head out of your ass and start to develop your own skillset. Your life will begin to change dramatically. Stop bitching and start hunting.

Pull out your notepad and a pencil and make a top-5 list of things you like doing. Next make a top-5 list of things you're good at doing. Finally, put together a top-5 list of things you've always imagined yourself doing. In that list of 15 things, I guarantee that you can find one thing worth developing. You may not have time to go back to school right now, but let me say this one thing to you that you may not have heard in a long time: "You're worth it." You're worth a continued education. Once you've identified something that's important to you. Something that gives you a larger purpose here on earth, you will need to get to the hard day-to-day work. Nick and I use daily journaling and goal setting to stay on track (more on that later). Especially with a busy schedule, it can be easy to put your personal development to the side and just deal with putting out the fires of daily life. You can't let that happen. You have to find a way to inch a little bit closer to your goals every week. Figure out what skillset you want to develop and how that fits in with your bigger purpose.

I went to film school right out of high school and it was the time of my life. I feel incredibly lucky that I was able to do something that I loved so much right out the gate. I feel even more blessed that I am able to use those skills to do the things that I love every day. But that wasn't always the case. I spent my early twenties serving drinks in tight clothes. Guess how I continued my education during that time? Online tutorials. With any skill you want to learn, there is an online tutorial for it. Stop pinning and start learning!

So take a break from digging through your ex's Instagram and put some time into developing your brain. Grab a cup of coffee and carve out 30 minutes for yourself at some point during the day. There is 1440 minutes in a day. Don't tell me that you don't have 30 minutes to yourself. If you get away from the TV and your smartphone, you will find time for developing your skills and your life. I can personally guarantee your life will change if you take time for your personal development. It's time to stop complaining and start putting forth a little elbow grease to get things done. I don't care if you're learning how to create a pumpkin spice rack from Martha Stewart on YOUTUBE, try some things you have never tried. Do something you have never done and make your time on this earth count. Finding purpose in this life will change everything. You will stop focusing on all the small and insignificant things. You will focus on your goals and your dreams. You will think about things like how you want to be remembered. You will feel invigorated and that basically makes it impossible to be a miserable cow.

#5. GET LAID

So, now you've changed your perspective and started to be grateful for the awesome life you've got. You've decided to relinquish control and let good things come into your life on your own. You're on the right track with nutrition and physical fitness and you're developing a new skill to

provide for yourself and your loved ones. You are
REALLY doing great! Now, it's time for some straight
talk… you need to get laid.

We all know the type: the prissy, prude, uppity princess
that snarls at men that look her way. The one with the
headphones and extremely high ponytail at the gym that
won't even glance in your direction. The uptight, stone-
cold bitch, who feels the need to address every flaw that
she can find within 10ft of your general direction. If she
actually decides to get married, her main concern will be
that her significant other sits up straight and plays nice in
an awkward engagement photo for the whole world to see
how she is able to control everything in her life. Every man
I've ever met knows exactly the type and has a sense of
urgency to "properly lay" a prissy stuck-up bitch like that
so she can finally let her hair down and enjoy a bottled beer
and some good music. It's a stereotype, but it is 100%
accurate. If you aren't enjoying a proper fuck on the
regular, it's likely that you are going to be annoyed with the
person you are spending ALL of your time with on a daily
basis. If you are withholding sex from your partner to
teach him or her a lesson you are missing out on life and

essentially setting yourself up for relational failure. Most miserable cows are likely NOT getting laid.

In our culture, women are told to be either sexual objects or prude, little girls. It's hard to find a natural in-between. Nobody is either or and that ends up messing us women up when it comes to sex. On top of that, a lot of women have some sort of baggage when it comes to their sexuality. My first husband ruined sex for me. It took me years to recover emotionally from his physical abuse. But I am so happy I got out on the other side so that I can enjoy sex again. A lot of women have experienced some sort of abuse and if you are one of them, you need to deal with it. It might even take some professional help, but you are going to thank yourself if you do the work. Other women have just been messed up by overly prude parents that told them that sex was a terrible and dirty thing, not a natural part of being human.

Regardless of the reason, it's time to get your groove back. Don't miss out on a mind-blowing orgasm just because your partner said something stupid at dinner. You are a couple. You both have needs. Don't use sex as a tool for manipulation. Don't use it to control him/her. It will just end up making your life sex-starved and miserable. If you want to create a bond that lasts and if you want to continue to enjoy life, you've got to let go of your frustrations and get laid! Here's the scientific reason why: When you orgasm you release the hormone oxytocin from nerve cells in the hypothalamus. Orgasms relieve tension and oxytocin stimulates feelings of warmth and relaxation. Intercourse was literally designed to create intimacy between you and your partner. On a more spiritual level, sex will be a way for you to enjoy life and cultivate fun and happiness. It's so simple so don't overthink it.

Alisa from **www.floliving.com** created the top 10 physical benefits of orgasm for women. Pay close attention:

1. Improves circulation to organs in the pelvic cavity, delivering nutrients, growing healthy tissues, and regulating your menstrual cycle. Women who have intercourse at least once a week are more likely to have normal menstrual cycles than women who are celibate or who have infrequent sex.

2. Increases fertility and your sense of wellness by energizing your hypothalamus gland, which regulates appetite, body temperature, emotions, and the pituitary gland, which in turn regulates the release of reproductive hormones that induce ovulation and cervical fluid.

3. Provides overall lymphatic massage, helping your body's natural detoxification process to improve digestion and mood and help prevent cancer.

4. Promotes healthy estrogen levels to keep vaginal tissues supple and protect against osteoporosis and heart disease.

5. Induces deep relaxation by boosting endorphin levels and flushing cortisol (an inflammatory hormone released by the adrenal glands) out of the body.

6. Spikes DHEA levels in the body. DHEA hormone improves brain function, balances the immune system, helps maintain and repair tissue, and promotes healthy skin.

7. Helps you look younger—studies show making love three times a week in a stress free relationship can make you look 10 years younger.

8. Boosts infection-fighting cells up to 20% – helps fight colds and the flu!

9. Cures migraines and helps treat other types of pain by elevating pain thresholds (a bonus when preparing for childbirth!)

10. Increases levels of the hormone oxytocin, which is linked to passion, intuition, and social skills—the hormone of bonding and success!

If you are miserable cow, you might need to read a list like that to make you slip into something a little less comfortable and get your sexy on. It can be hard to get back into the game if you and your significant other have been going through a drought. If you are struggling with you libido or even your feelings towards your current partner, I suggest getting with a doctor who can tell if your hormones are the reason and help you to get your body back on track. But before you start blaming it all on hormones, just try to think back to the beginning of your relationship. How did you feel towards your significant other? What did you do to feel sexy? You might just need to stop complaining, get out of your granny panties, put on some music and seduce the hell out of your mate. They might be a little shocked at first, but I am sure they will appreciate it. If you're not in a relationship, get off your couch and start dating. I'm not saying you need to sign up on Tinder and pursue a life of one-night stands, but get out there and find a good one. Personally, my love language is physical touch. So for me, having a partner that is interested and willing is one of the biggest blessings on the planet. Don't miss out on life. Don't settle for a sexless life. Get laid. It's awesome.

#6. SET GOALS

Your miserable cow is looking pretty dead at this point. It's time for the final cut to really make sure it's gone. In other words, it's time to make a plan of action to attack the things you want to accomplish.

First, I have a confession to make: most of my life I have found myself floating through life, seemingly chasing my own tail and trying to keep my head above water. It's a problem I have. I get involved in too many things and I lose track. Nick and I own and run multiple businesses and a non-profit. I have never worked more in my entire life. From the moment our feet hit the floor in the morning until we break for the gym in the evening, we are working. And I am not quite sure anyone even understands what it is exactly we do... (but I will get to that.) At some point, I started to feel like I was getting nowhere. Kicking my hardest to get out to sea only to realize that tide was coming in and I was going to be KOOK SLAMMED into the shore with my bikini top hanging around my waist. My work life is incredibly rewarding, but it is also extremely taxing. It is so important to be authentic and the most ingenious version of myself at all times. In order for me to be the free-spirit girl with the big heart and passion for life,

I have to have my shit together. Otherwise, I'm just the scattered girl who likes to spend money on travel and takes a lot of selfies. In order to stay on track, I needed a better plan. With my whole heart I desired to write this book, have a podcast, get in great physical shape, have healthy relationships and travel the world. That's it. No big deal right? Time and time again, Nick has watched me struggling to feel like I was accomplishing anything for myself. I would get cranky and bitchy because I was mad at myself for not making any time for myself. I poured my life into work that was definitely meaningful, but not getting me closer to some of my personal goals so I needed help. One day in our office he came to me with a small cardboard box. All I could think was that I hoped it was snacks. But luckily for me, it was something far more precious: a journal. To some, the gesture might seem insignificant, but I knew exactly what it meant. He knows how much I love to write. He knows how much I believe in the power of positivity and expression. He knew I needed a jumpstart.

I would highly recommend getting yourself a journal. It will be a place to record your goals and a place to make sure that you stay on track. **Best Self Co** makes an excellent one. Nick and I crack open our journals over coffee every morning. This specific journal truly has the potential to crack the code on life, especially if you're a scatterbrained artist, such as myself. Not only do you write down your goals each day, you will also write down the steps you will need to take to move you closer to your goals. You have a complete 13-week calendar plan of how to get you where you want to be. Additionally, every morning you list three things you are thankful for in the present. And every night you access what big wins you had for the day and what lessons you've learned. It's truly life changing. With a journal routine, you will be able to see exactly where you are, where you have been and where you want to go. It is a way to empower yourself. I like that I share this activity with Nick, but you don't have to convince your significant other to get on board with this. Although, I know he or she would benefit as well. This is something you are going to do for yourself. And something you will thank yourself for when you start seeing results and start feeling like you are finally moving forward in life.

Maybe your goal is to organize your family. From start to finish you've got to write a plan of how you're going to get more organized. Maybe your goal is to get in better shape. Take a deep breath and write out what you want to do every day to bring yourself closer to that goal. Want to stop being a miserable cow? Make your visions a reality by setting goals.

Hair Messy #eyessparkling

#7. GET OFF YOUR ASS

One of my favorite quotes. *"And at the end of the day, your feet should be dirty, your hair messy and your eyes sparkling."* - Shanti

Sometimes the most effective way to deal with feeling miserable is to force yourself to do something outside of your comfort zone. To adventure a little. Personally I can't express to you enough how much the outdoors does for my soul. I grew up running around barefoot in the woods of Missouri. My hair was always messy and my eyes were always sparkling. My mom tried her best to make me a presentable girl, but I was always the little girl covered in dirt, in the field behind the church on Sundays, flying over fences in a dress with tears in my dirty stockings and mud on my patent leathers. I couldn't help it. I lived in trees and my toes loved mud. As a teenager my parents sent me on missions trip to 3rd world countries. Dirt floors, cold showers, and barracks style sleeping outdoors in the jungles of Brazil with dinner plate sized spiders and bats flying overhead… and I think I loved it more than anything I had ever done. So maybe my idea of adventures is a little different than yours. Nonetheless if you want to kill the misery… it's time to do something different. It's time to adventure. As often as you can.

So I talked about my marriages and I talked about raising kids. But nothing hurt worse than making the decision to move away from my boys and start over. Before my thirtieth birthday I was going through some of the hardest times of my life. I always thought I would be celebrating my thirties with loads of friends, having the time of my life. But it wasn't that way things turned out for me. I was in the middle of my SECOND divorce, separating from my stepchildren and working 70 hours a week to keep my head above water. I remember wishing every day that my life would fast forward, that each day would pass faster because I was so miserable. I felt so empty without my stepsons in my life every day. It was a huge transition to part ways after never being without them more than a day in 6 years. I cried myself to sleep almost every night. I knew I couldn't be with their dad anymore because he refused to get better. After a year of separation and trying to co-parent as a stepparent, it was obvious we were pro-longing the inevitable. The boys and their dad wanted me back full time. I spent every evening during the week at the house making them dinner and helping with homework. I would tuck my youngest into bed and head to my mom's for the night. I woke up before the sun was up to go wake them up and get them ready for school. I am sure it was extremely confusing for them and it wasn't what I ever intended. He didn't want me to tell them we were getting divorced, because he didn't want to get divorced. When I tried to explain to them what was going on, he would go behind my back and tell them that he knew I was coming home and that they just needed to pray and believe. I didn't know exactly how to handle it. My friends all told me that I had to file the paperwork, make it official, cut ties etc. But my heart was bleeding out. I wanted to stay in their lives. I wanted to take them with me. But it all came down to one thing. They weren't mine. I didn't give birth to them, they didn't have my name. I lost. I struggled the worst around holidays. I hated everything about these days. I just wanted them to be over. I felt like the universe treated me unfairly. Like I had been given a bad hand. Life was hard and unfair and nothing I had worked for had panned out.

There is no "quick fix" or epiphany that I can give you to go through the horrible things in life. But the truth was, I made choices. Choices every single day that either perpetuated my condition of misery or propelled me forward into my passions, gave me renewed hope.

Sometimes it just takes time. But we each make daily choices that can waste our life and keep us miserable OR, they send us in a new direction. Remember how I said that Nick and I couldn't have met at a worse time? This is why. I was going through sooo much transition. I was going through the worst pain I had ever felt in my life. Separating from my boys was eating away at me from the inside out. I was a mess, and Nick seemed like a good time. Well, he was a good time. But lucky for me, he was so much more.

This isn't a love story by the way, this isn't a book about landing the man of your dreams. I just want to clarify that. This is a story about making it through personal pain, forgiving yourself, walking through the fire and coming out on the other side.

Oh how my life has changed. I set goals and then I accomplish them. I put forth effort every single day to develop myself. When I met Nick, my world was turned upside down. Never have I ever been so motivated to enjoy life. The challenges he faced before the military are something that I think very few of us would have overcome. Every bit of adversity only made him MORE motivated to succeed. Rewind to our generation's "War on Terror" and "Enduring Freedom" and we are talking about scores of friends lost, hurt or emotionally damaged seemingly beyond repair. And while some combat veterans use this trauma as an excuse to withdraw or drink themselves to sleep every night, he hated where that was taking him. Nick was motivated. He was motived to get better. His transition was brutal, but getting to the other side motivated him to live life to the fullest. He was motivated to make every day count. It puts everything into perspective to have someone like that in your life.

As my boys have turned in to teenagers I have tried to stay as connected in their lives as I can. Writing them, calling them, sending them care packages. The oldest are 18 and 19 years old. If they want to keep a relationship with me, ultimately, they have decisions to make too. We all go through hard things. It's how we choose to live thereafter that defines us. Nick challenged me to give up my wallowing... let go of my pain, forgive myself and look forward to a promising future full of life. I had to GET OFF MY ASS!

Sometimes it is as simple as trying something new. A new cardio class, a business networking group, video editing tutorials. Whether it is something to better yourself, develop a skill set or further your business, it can be just what you need! Bottom line: if you want to give the miserable cow that final blow, you need to get out there and an adventure often so that you keep growing and don't get stuck in a rut again.

This year I celebrated my 33rd birthday with the people I love trying something new: SNOWBOARDING. It's challenging to learn something new this late in the game. For someone who likes riding bikes and lifting heavy weights the free-fluid movements for something like snowboarding never came naturally to me. The first time we went, I destroyed my neck. I busted my ass more times then I can count. But, I refused to give up. Well, Nick refused to let me give up. Second time was amazing. I took a lesson and actually enjoyed the hell out of every minute.

Next new activity of this year was climbing. I've always been a climber. I love being up high and I love pushing my body going up trees, mountains and rocks. I am consciously working towards sharpening my skills. Now I'm on to long-boarding. Every day I spend time on my longboard, practicing balance and learning to let go of fear and enjoy myself, I feel how the adventures are making me a happier person. Activity for some might just be activity. But for me, the process of pushing myself through physical challenges and adventures has been healing. Maybe for you it isn't a physical challenge. Maybe for you it is an emotional one like going to speak to a friend you had a falling out with, choosing to forgive and making the effort to heal. Maybe it's writing a book! Telling your story can be the most cathartic thing you ever do.

The truth is that you can't fast forward the hard times. But I promise you this. If you decide to get off your A$$ and make everyday count, you will grow and enjoy life a little more everyday. Even through the most challenging weeks, you have the opportunity to make a choice to go on even the smallest adventure. Maybe it's just a trip to a new restaurant, trying yoga in the park for the first time, or a lesson in stand up paddle boarding. Who cares what exactly it is because the point is that you can always choose to spice your life with some adventure. Even when everything else sucks, this can be a way to find a sliver of happiness. Get outside, put some wind in your hair. Put your feet in the earth and do something you've never done.

Maybe you can't go anywhere just yet. Get out the dog leash, take your kids to the park. Stop scrolling and start strolling. Find a list of free events in the local paper. Get some cash out and go to the city market. Put your hair up and go for a jog.

Your body's frequency at perfect peace is the very same as that of the earth. Most people don't know it, but frequency has the ability to affect your body either positively or negatively. Some electromagnetic energies generated by computers, cellphones and electronic devices contain energy codes or frequencies that don't synchronize and harmonize well with your body. So how do you get your body back to peace and calm? Grounding. It may sound strange, but simply walking barefoot outside with your the soles of your feet touching the earth for 15-30 minutes a day can help with inflammation, reduce stress and overall help you sleep better. Your next adventure can start by just ditching your shoes!

Ok, as I promised this still isn't a love story, so stay with me for a minute. Do you know what I hate more than people who poop with the door open? I mean, we are talking 'the people walking past you with purpose because they know exactly where they need to be and why...' and they breeze right past the bathroom door as though it doesn't exist or worse somehow its presence is arbitrary to them; and they de-pants themselves, pop a squat and shit. With the door open. They might possibly even call to you down the hall to come talk to them... WHILE THEY ARE SHITTING! Yes, so there is only one thing I hate more than those people and that is lying to myself. Proving

myself wrong. I try not to make blanket or black and white statements that lock me in or pigeon hole me. I learned at a very young age that my absolutes were frequently disproven, quite often by myself. "I hate _____."
Then, 2 years later, I decide I really like _____. I may not have hated _____ before... Maybe I just didn't know enough about _____ to make a decision about _____ so hastily. Or maybe the mix-up was simple. Maybe I just changed my mind. I hate lying to myself because it usually means that I took a stand on something that I shouldn't have. I want to stay open to everything in life and when I'm proving myself wrong it means there was an element in my life that I wasn't open-minded about. Anyway, I was recently proven wrong about one of the big NEVER WILL I EVER parts of my life.

Koumalatsos Wedding 10.2.18 #FuckFear

I got married for the first time at 19, mostly because I wanted to have my entire life mapped out before I started living it. Seems strange right, I am a free-spirit, artistic, gypsy right? SURE. Well, the truth is, as much as I love to travel, enjoy life, pack light, get super dirty and wear bright orange.... I also really like to be in control of ME. I enjoy feeling like I am in charge of the direction the wind blows me. Welp, lesson learned. We are **NEVER** in charge. God, the Universe, LIFE - whatever you want to call it - lets us make choices, but also lets other individuals make choices and those are sometimes bad choices - that end up affecting us. Sometimes, things just happen that will be outside of our control. Just like a public shitter.

Anyway, I got married at 19 and it ended as many people might have expected: terribly. And as I told you in the very beginning, I was in a physically and emotionally abusive relationship before I understood what that meant. And without hesitation I jumped into relationships right after that were equally dysfunctional. I told myself it would all be ok and that I just wouldn't get married again. But then, as I told you in the middle of the book, I did. And even worse than the first, that one ended so painfully because I hurt everyone involved. So, that was it for me. The last straw. "I'm NEVER getting married again!" I never want to hurt anyone else, I don't want to fail anymore. I told myself that it just isn't for me. It took some time, but I had completely convinced myself that this was the way things HAD to be for a "person like me."

Mexico #MyLove

Enter Nick. I thought I had done it. I thought I had the perfect solution to all of my problems. A "fun-time" guy. Someone I could have fun with, be friends with, and just keep things light. The perfect person to remain "un-attached" with. The ultimate oxymoron. The only flaw in my formula is that I didn't take in to consideration that maybe I had met my match; I would fall in love and quite possibly have found my partner for life. We spent months talking and getting to know each other as friends. When we actually met in person we had an amazing connection. As I'm writing this book, the last four years have flown by. There hasn't been a full 24 hours that we've gone without talking to each other, or communicating in some way. We've had the worst fights. Gone through our own personal hells together and established an armory of our past baggage that we can draw from for any fight. And through it all, he's still my person. I've grown to understand more about forgiveness and love because of him. And I'm certain that he is pushing me to be the best version of myself that I could ever be.

When Nick got down on one knee (well, actually it was both knees because he's broken lol) I was absolutely SHOCKED. We had always said we would NEVER get married. He had his own reasons. Then we started saying, well, maybe someday. I had no idea what he was planning for our little celebration trip to Mexico. The first words out of my mouth were... "Are you sure?!" Because we didn't plan on this. I was fearful because of all of my issues in my past. And the part of me that wanted to be in charge of everything was freaking out. I have been through a lot of shit. I have been the most miserable of cows. But I am not going to let that hold me back. Maybe the biggest adventure of all for me is the one of facing my biggest fear.

I'm not saying that you HAVE to get married. You DON'T have everything figured out, so don't always pretend that you do. Your story isn't all-the-way written. There are many more chapters to come. You determine the ending in the little choices you make every single day. Choices to be positive, see the best in everyone, forgive, let go and move forward. Choices to leave your past behind and embrace what's in front of you. DON'T BE A MISERABLE COW! AND NEVER SAY NEVER! PHOTO

I told you I would get back to the "what we do" part. I am sure people look at my Instagram and think: "what a pretentious little brat. She's gallivanting around the world, taking pictures and videos." I sometimes ask myself why people even care what my husband and I are doing. And truth is, I don't know! It feels sort of surreal that we get to do the things we do, especially if you were able to take a look at our bank account. Nick and I have created a YOUTUBE channel for all of his adventures. Starring him as the online personality. I like to think of him as a guide. We produce each episode ourselves. I shoot and edit, create content and promote the channel. In the first year we gained over 25 thousands subscribers and it seems to grow more everyday. We just hit 120K subscribers recently. We spend our time on the road and keeping up with just about every opportunity that is thrown our way. We are able to do this because of our sponsors and because of all the hard work and efforts we put forth on the side to keep the ship moving. It takes a lot of hard work behind the scenes, and both flexibility and sacrifice. We didn't start this way, we sort of happened upon it and I can tell you it is truly amazing. It was outside of our comfort zone and we didn't really foresee the success of it. But we were passionate and serious about it and that attracted subscribers and sponsors. It works out wonderfully for a gypsy like me – I adventure with my significant other for a living and I work to inspire and motivate others through the artistic content we create.

The Best is Yet to Come #LiveFree

KILL THE COW

So there you have it. If the miserable cow isn't dead by now then you might just need to buy more cats, and get on a really good cable plan because you're doomed. We have covered some very important things in this book. By no means do I have it all together. I make things look great because I am a photographer. BUT NOTHING IS EVER PERFECT. Nothing is even close. But I have determined to enjoy my life no matter what anyone else around me is doing.

Do you want to live your life to the fullest and enjoy it no matter what anyone else around you is choosing?

Everyday I think about the free-spirited chick I saw in the mirror when I was 16. Is she still in there? You want to get rid of resting bitch face? You want to be **CONTENT?**

STOP comparing yourself to others.

Get some perspective.

BE thankful for everything you have.

STOP letting everyone offend you. **FORGIVE.**

FIND your passion and vision, make a plan.

Set some **GOALS.**

Get healthy. **DEVELOP** yourself.

STOP being critical of others.

FOCUS on your own shit.

ADVENTURE OFTEN

YOU DON'T HAVE TO BE A MISERABLE COW.

YOU are in charge of your happiness and peace. You have the power to pursue **HAPPINESS**, to find **LOVE**, and to **LIVE THE LIFE YOU WANT.**

Tune in to my podcast:
How NOT to be a Miserable Cow

ABOUT THE AUTHOR

Alison Capra is a writer, producer, and creator devoted to telling the stories that take her behind the scenes, off the grid, and up the next mountain. Alison spent the last 18 years traveling the world and experiencing new cultures. Her passion is for the outdoors, people, and art in all forms.

Alison is a film school graduate from Full Sail University. She a partner of Alexander Industries in Eastern North, Carolina with her husband Nick Koumalatsos. Together they produce a successful YOUTUBE channel, and a podcast.

CPSIA information can be obtained
at www.ICGtesting.com
Printed in the USA
BVHW040038171120
593460BV00027B/567